CHAPTER ONE: SELF-HARM AND SUICIDE

Suicide

Why is it that some people feel suicidal? What pushes someone to suicide? Figures for 1999 suggest that there are as many as 20,000 suicide attempts made by young people a year

There are a number of significant events in people's lives that can make them more prone to suicide. These include being treated abusively, being harassed or bullied, a breakdown in the family or relationships or a bereavement, as well as depression and other kinds of mental illness. Having someone to talk to regularly is also important.

Suicide and attempted suicide are often linked to a build-up, or combination of difficult events. There might also be a 'last straw' event that encourages someone to attempt suicide. Not everyone who feels suicidal actually attempts to kill himself or herself. But if they do it can be a desperate call for help.

It used to be said that people who talk about suicide don't actually attempt it. Statistics have shown, however, that this is not the case. If you are feeling suicidal it may seem almost impossible to find something to look forward to beyond your current situation. This makes it seem impossible to sort things out. You may feel that other people don't understand your situation.

If you know someone who is feeling suicidal it is important to take his or her feelings seriously. You could find out what professional help is available and encourage the person to take it up. It is also important to be aware of your own limitations. It might be that you don't feel you are able to listen to the person at certain times or even at all. It is better to be honest than being unrealistic with the person about what you can offer. Make them aware that there are trained counsellors and advisers who can listen to what they have to say however bleak and hard their situation may seem.

If someone you know closely or someone in your family has committed suicide and you don't have family or friends to support you, you may also want to talk to a trained counsellor. Youth Access (Tel: 0208 772 9900) will refer you to a young person's counselling service in your area or you could speak to an organisation like Cruse Bereavement Care which specialises in bereavement counselling.

Unlike a natural death, when someone commits suicide the police will be involved and there will be an inquest into the death. *The Work of the Coroner*, published by the Home Office, explains the work of the Coroner and what happens at an inquest. It is available free of charge from the Home Office on: 020 7273 3776.

Young men and suicide

Suicide is three times as common in men than women and the number of suicides among young men has increased dramatically over the last 10 years. Suicide and undetermined injury accounts for almost 20% of all deaths among young men between the ages of 15 and 24. In 1996 it accounted for over 450 deaths in the UK It is the second most common cause of death; road traffic accidents is the highest.

A recent ChildLine report suggests that only 1 in 4 of the calls they receive are from boys. Girls are far more likely to call for help and

> *If you know someone who is feeling suicidal it is important to take his or her feelings seriously*

THERE IS HELP!

when boys finally do call their problems are amongst the most severe that ChildLine deals with. Another Helpline has been set up aimed exclusively at trying to help young men cope with suicidal feelings. It is called CALM (Campaign Against Living Miserably). They want to hear from you if you are between the ages of 15 and 24 and are feeling miserable or worried and want to talk it through. The helpline is open between 5pm and 8am. They will also put you in touch with local support groups run through the NHS or by voluntary organisations.

Although more young women attempt suicide, three times as many young men actually kill themselves. The reasons aren't entirely clear but one factor may be that some young men find it very difficult to express their feelings, with the result that emotions build up to breaking point inside. Young men may find it more difficult to ask for assistance.

Some young men find it very difficult to express their feelings, with the result that emotions build up to breaking point inside. Young men may find it more difficult to ask for assistance

---

Outside factors such as high levels of youth unemployment, poor housing and heavy use of alcohol and drugs may also increase the risk of suicide.

Although the number of young women who actually kill themselves is less, an attempted suicide is still a very clear indication that something is wrong and it is important that it is taken seriously.

There are several useful books on suicide that you could find in a bookshop or library. Mind produces a free booklet on suicide called *How to Help Someone Who is Suicidal*. The Samaritans produce a free booklet on men and suicide that includes information on how to cope with suicidal feelings.

■ The above information is from www.younginformation.com
© 2000 National Youth Agency

Self-directed violence

Information from the World Health Organization

Suicide is one of the leading causes of death worldwide and is an important public health problem. Among those aged 15-44 years, self-inflicted injuries are the fourth leading cause of death and the sixth leading cause of ill-health and disability.

In much of the world, suicide is stigmatised and condemned for religious or cultural reasons. In some countries, suicidal behaviour is a criminal offence punishable by law. Suicide is therefore often a secretive act surrounded by taboo, and may be unrecognised, misclassified or deliberately hidden in official records of death.

The extent of the problem
■ An estimated 815,000 people killed themselves in 2000 – a rate of 14.5 per 100,000 or roughly one death every 40 seconds.
■ The highest rates of suicide in the world are found in Eastern European countries. The lowest rates are found mainly in Latin America and a few countries in Asia.
■ Within countries, suicide rates

are frequently higher among indigenous groups – notable examples include the Aboriginal and Torres Strait Islander populations in Australia and the Inuit in Canada's Arctic north.
■ In general, suicide rates increase with age. Rates among people aged 60 and older are about three times the rates among people 15-29 years of age. The absolute numbers are, however, higher among those below 45 years of age.

■ Even though women are more prone to suicidal thoughts than men, rates of suicide are higher among men. On average, there are about three male suicides for every female one – though in parts of Asia, the ratio is much narrower.
■ Suicidal thoughts and attempts are common among young people. The ratio of attempts to completed suicides among people under 25 years of age may reach as high as 100-200:1.
■ In general, about 10% of people who attempt suicide eventually kill themselves.

What are the risk factors for self-directed violence?
A variety of stressful events or circumstances can put people at increased risk of harming themselves including the loss of loved ones, interpersonal conflicts with family or friends and legal or work-related problems. To act as precipitating factors for suicide, though, they must happen to someone who is pre-disposed or otherwise especially vulnerable to self-harm.

CONTENTS

Chapter One: Self-harm and Suicide

Chapter Two: Seeking Help

Introduction

Self-inflicted Violence is the seventy-seventh volume in the **Issues** series. The aim of this series is to offer up-to-date information about important issues in our world.

Self-inflicted Violence looks at the issues of suicide and self-harm and how to seek help.

The information comes from a wide variety of sources and includes:
Government reports and statistics
Newspaper reports and features
Magazine articles and surveys
Web site material
Literature from lobby groups
and charitable organisations.

It is hoped that, as you read about the many aspects of the issues explored in this book, you will critically evaluate the information presented. It is important that you decide whether you are being presented with facts or opinions. Does the writer give a biased or an unbiased report? If an opinion is being expressed, do you agree with the writer?

Self-inflicted Violence offers a useful starting-point for those who need convenient access to information about the many issues involved. However, it is only a starting-point. At the back of the book is a list of organisations which you may want to contact for further information.

*****

Predisposing factors include:
- alcohol and drug abuse
- a history of physical or sexual abuse in childhood
- social isolation
- psychiatric problems such as mood disorders, schizophrenia and a general sense of hopelessness.

Other significant factors include:
- having access to the means to kill oneself (most typically guns, medicines and agricultural poisons)
- physical illnesses, especially those that are painful or disabling
- having made a previous suicide attempt.

Certain social and environmental factors also increase the likelihood of suicide. Rates of suicide, for instance, are higher during economic recessions and periods of high unemployment. They are also higher during periods of social disintegration, political instability and social collapse.

What can be done to prevent self-directed violence?

Treatment of mental disorders

The early identification and appropriate treatment of mental disorders is an important prevention strategy – especially given the relevant contribution of depression and other psychiatric problems to suicidal behaviour. Equally important is early identification and treatment for people with alcohol- and substance-abuse problems.

Behavioural approaches

People who are suicidal generally express difficulty in solving problems. Behavioural therapy approaches are designed to probe underlying factors and to help patients develop problem-solving skills. While conclusive answers are not yet known, there is some evidence to suggest that behavioural therapy approaches are effective in reducing suicidal thoughts and behaviour.

Community-based efforts

Local communities are important settings for suicide prevention activities. Some of the more common measures include:

- suicide prevention centres that offer telephone hotlines, counselling, and outreach
- community-based programmes in youth centres and centres for older people
- support groups for people who have attempted suicide as well as for family members and friends who have lost someone to suicide
- media and other educational campaigns to raise awareness of the problem and reduce the taboo attached to suicidal behaviour.

School-based interventions are important for reaching young people. While school staff cannot replace mental health professionals, they can be trained to identify the signs and symptoms of suicidal behaviour and refer those at risk to appropriate mental health services. Educational programmes for students can also be beneficial.

Social and environmental strategies

A major factor determining whether suicidal behaviour will be fatal or not is the method chosen. Shooting, jumping from a height and hanging are among the most lethal methods of suicide.

Reducing access to the means of self-harm is thus an important prevention strategy and one that has proved effective. Notable reductions in suicide have occurred, for instance, in countries that have removed carbon monoxide from domestic gas and car exhausts or restricted access to concentrated agricultural poisons among people. Restrictions on the ownership of firearms have been associated with a decrease of their use for suicide.

- For more information, please visit: http://www.who.int/violence_injury_prevention

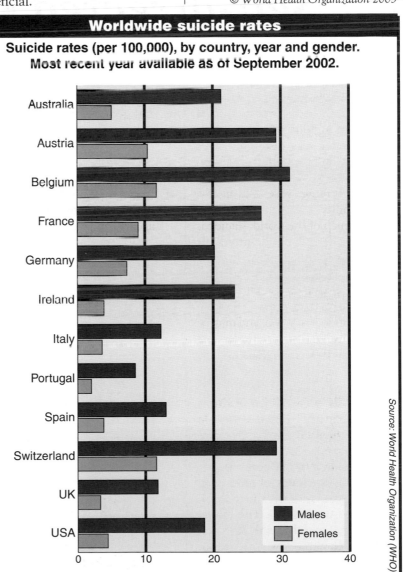

Worldwide suicide rates

Suicide rates (per 100,000), by country, year and gender. Most recent year available as of September 2002.

Australia, Austria, Belgium, France, Germany, Ireland, Italy, Portugal, Spain, Switzerland, UK, USA

Males / Females

0 10 20 30 40

Source: World Health Organization (WHO)

The warning signs of suicide

Suicide is rarely a spur-of-the-moment decision. In the days and hours before people kill themselves, there are usually clues and warning signs.

The strongest and most disturbing signs are verbal – 'I can't go on,' 'Nothing matters any more' or even 'I'm thinking of ending it all.' Such remarks should always be taken seriously.

Other common warning signs include:

- Becoming depressed or withdrawn
- Behaving recklessly
- Getting affairs in order and giving away valued possessions
- Showing a marked change in behaviour, attitudes or appearance
- Abusing drugs or alcohol
- Suffering a major loss or life change

The following list gives more examples, all of which can be signs that somebody is contemplating suicide. Of course, in most cases these situations do not lead to suicide. But, generally, the more signs a person displays, the higher the risk of suicide.

Situations

- Family history of suicide or violence
- Sexual or physical abuse
- Death of a close friend or family member
- Divorce or separation, ending a relationship
- Failing academic performance, impending exams, exam results
- Job loss, problems at work
- Impending legal action
- Recent imprisonment or upcoming release

Behaviours

- Crying
- Fighting
- Breaking the law
- Impulsiveness
- Self-mutilation
- Writing about death and suicide
- Previous suicidal behaviour
- Extremes of behaviour
- Changes in behaviour

Physical changes

- Lack of energy
- Disturbed sleep patterns – sleeping too much or too little
- Loss of appetite
- Sudden weight gain or loss
- Increase in minor illnesses
- Change of sexual interest
- Sudden change in appearance
- Lack of interest in appearance

Thoughts and emotions

- Thoughts of suicide
- Loneliness – lack of support from family and friends
- Rejection, feeling marginalised
- Deep sadness or guilt
- Unable to see beyond a narrow focus
- Daydreaming
- Anxiety and stress
- Helplessness
- Loss of self-worth

■ The above information is from the site of former Befrienders International (now maintained by Samaritans).

© *Befrienders International*

Suicide

Information from ChildLine

Feelings of despair, isolation and hopelessness can affect anyone of any age, at any time. When these feelings become too much to bear, it can seem to some young people that suicide is the only way to escape their problems.

Some facts and figures about suicide

- There are at least two suicides every day by young people under the age of 25 in the UK and Republic of Ireland
- In the UK the suicide rate in young men (aged 15-24 years) is 17 per

100,000 compared with the national suicide rate of 13 per 100,000
- In the Republic of Ireland, suicide amongst young men continues to rise dramatically and in 1997 was 27 per 100,000; three times the rate for 1987
- It is estimated that there are

approximately 19,000 suicide attempts by adolescents every year, which is more than one every 30 minutes
- Young women aged between 15 and 19 years are the most likely to attempt suicide, usually by overdose. However the rate amongst young men has nearly tripled since 1985

What causes some young people to feel suicidal?

There is no simple explanation for suicidal behaviour. Calls to ChildLine show that abuse, constant rows with someone close, bullying, stress over exams, and worries about the future are just some of the things that, in some young people, can cause feelings of anxiety, low self-esteem, hopelessness and isolation. This can lead to thoughts of suicide. Groups particularly at risk of suicide include unemployed or homeless young people, young gay men and women, and young people who have problems with drugs.

Depression and despair can also be caused by specific events, such as the death of someone, parents splitting up, unwanted pregnancy, a relationship ending, or a violent incident such as rape. Sometimes young people, like adults, can feel deeply unhappy for no obvious reason at all, and believe that they will feel that way for ever.

What do young people tell ChildLine about feeling suicidal?

Some young people who talk to ChildLine about feeling suicidal have actually made an attempt – such as an overdose – just before calling, and need immediate medical help. Others are feeling so unhappy about problems in their lives that they say or imply they are thinking of killing themselves. Some have felt depressed for a long time, while others are reacting to a recent event. Some have only just started thinking about suicide, but others have already made suicide attempts in the past. Although, deep down, many of the young people who call ChildLine feeling suicidal may not really want to die, they tell us that at the time death feels like the only way of dealing with their problems. They find it hard to look at other options, and often feel that no other solution will work. Their self-esteem may be so low that they believe they are a burden, and that their family, or the world, would be happier and better off without them. They may believe that people around them will be 'punished' by their death.

How do ChildLine counsellors help young people who feel suicidal?

Just picking up the phone and ringing ChildLine is an important step for a young person to take. Talking, being

'Six weeks ago a friend of mine took an overdose. She was under a lot of pressure and couldn't tell anybody. She said she really wanted to die and wouldn't let me phone for an ambulance or call her parents . . . so I called ChildLine.

'I'd just like to say how brilliant they were. They talked to her and stayed on the phone while the ambulance was coming, and also helped me afterwards. I never believed that ChildLine could be so helpful but they saved my friend's life.'

Letter to magazine problem page

listened to and being taken seriously can make all the difference between a young person choosing to live or die. Callers often tell ChildLine how important it was for them to have someone who took the time to listen, to try to understand how they are feeling, and to be there for them at a time of crisis in their lives. While taking seriously the young person's thought of suicide, ChildLine counsellors also help them to work out what has contributed to their depression, and look with them at ways of changing or coping with their situation. Callers are encouraged to talk about any feelings of pain, loss, anger and unhappiness, without being judged. Counsellors help callers feel valued, and build up their confidence and sense of self-worth. Thoughts of suicide may take time to subside, or recur later, so callers are encouraged to call back, or get support from someone close. Counsellors can also offer practical help, like giving information about support available in the young person's area, such as face-to-face counselling. If a caller's life is in immediate danger, for example from an overdose of tablets, counsellors will get help from the emergency services.

Some more facts about suicide

- People who make suicide attempts or threats are not just 'attention seeking', but are at risk of harming themselves.
- Anyone who talks about killing himself or herself, or tries to do it, is deeply unhappy, and needs help.
- Most suicidal people are undecided about living or dying, and try beforehand to let others know how they are feeling, or give clues and warnings.
- Talking about suicide with someone will not make them more likely to harm themselves.
- Every year around 2,000 children and young people talk to Child-Line about feeling suicidal.

Contacting ChildLine

Children can call ChildLine on 0800 1111 (all calls are free of charge, 24 hours a day, 365 days a year).

Or write to us at ChildLine, Freepost NATN1111, London E1 6BR; or visit www.childline.org.uk Children who are deaf or find using a regular phone difficult can try our textphone service on 0800 400 222. Monday to Friday 9.30am to 9.30pm. Saturday to Sunday 9.30am to 8.00pm.

We have a special helpline for children and young people living away from home in places like refuges, boarding schools and young offenders' institutions called The Line on 0800 88 444. Monday to Friday 9.30am to 9.30pm. Saturday to Sunday 9.30am to 8.00pm. ChildLine in Partnership with Schools (CHIPS) helps schools set up schemes to encourage children and young people to support each other. For more information call 020 7650 3231.   © ChildLine

Girls who cut

Self-harm is increasing among children as young as six. Hilary Freeman reports on why so many are turning to the razor, and one teenager tells her story

Paula is 12. She doesn't get on with her parents because they dislike her friends and complain that she stays out too late. Lately, they have been having huge, ugly rows which leave Paula feeling angry and upset. She will go to her room and take the razor she uses to shave her legs out of the drawer. Then she will drag it along her wrists or upper arms, cutting deep into the flesh until her blood pours. It makes her feel better, less angry and raw.

Her friends know she does it and understand why. Several of them cut themselves too.

What is most shocking about Paula's story is not that she regularly mutilates her body but that in doing so she is not unusual. For girls like her – and less commonly, boys – self-harm is a normal, almost banal response to emotional pain. In September 2003, the BBC Six O'Clock News released the results of a survey of 50 accident and emergency departments, which found that 66% of staff believed cases of child and adolescent self-harm were increasing.

They reported seeing an average of 13 cases per month, with one department reporting three a day. More worryingly, most thought the age of self-harmers was falling. The average age of those treated was just 11, but children as young as six were admitted with self-inflicted injuries.

Since hospitals only see cases which require medical attention, the true number of child self-harmers must be countless times higher. Earlier this year, the Samaritans commissioned a study of teenage self-harm, conducted by the Centre for Suicide Research at Oxford University. After quizzing 6,000 teenagers it concluded that more than one in 10 adolescents have deliberately cut themselves at some time. Girls were almost four times as likely as boys to do so. Only 13% of self-harm incidents had led to a hospital visit.

These statistics do not surprise me. As an agony aunt for the teenage magazine *CosmoGIRL!*, I receive between five and 20 letters and emails each week which either mention or allude to self-harm. In most of these letters, from girls aged between 15 and 17, self-harm is not seen as the primary problem. Often it is mentioned halfway down the letter, almost as an afterthought.

'It's hard to be sure if teenage self-harm really is on the increase or whether we're just more aware of it now, looking for it and asking the right questions so we find it'

One girl said she couldn't cope with the pressure of choosing between several different sixth forms and asked me to help her decide which one to pick. Later she mentioned that the stress was making her 'feel like I want to cut myself, which I haven't done in a year'. Another detailed her experience of bullying, before revealing that her coping mechanism was to cut herself with scissors.

If, like me, you cringe at the mere thought of tearing off a plaster or pulling out a splinter, the concept of slicing or burning your own skin deliberately in order to cause injury and pain seems both abhorrent and alien. How can so many young people find it so easy to hurt themselves?

According to Dr Michaela Swales, a lecturer practitioner in clinical psychology at the University of Wales, the answer is that self-harming is not as far from normal behaviour as we might believe. 'Cutting oneself is simply an unhealthy habit, not that different from drowning one's sorrows in a few drinks, drug taking or smoking cigarettes to relieve stress,' she says. 'Rationally, we know that smoking is bad for our health and will harm us in the long term. But in the short term it makes us feel better, so we do it. It's the same for those who cut themselves.'

Swales says children and teenagers who cut themselves do not necessarily have mental health problems: 'There are many and varied reasons why people self-harm, but broadly there are three explanations. The first category describes young people who use cutting as a way of coping with a situation, as a way of releasing tension or changing an

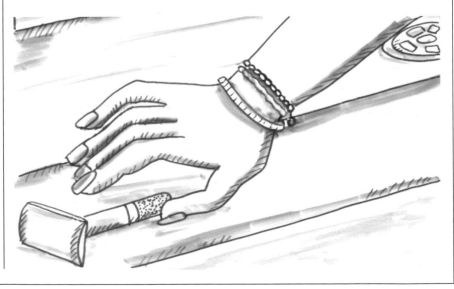

unpleasant emotional state. For some, physical pain is more bearable than emotional pain.

'Second, some young people use self-harm to give them a sense of control over a situation which they can't control, such as bullying for example.

'Finally, self-harm is used by some young people as a way of validating their suffering. A child who has been abused may feel that nobody believes them because they don't show any visible marks. By harming themselves they create a physical manifestation of their inner pain.'

Experts are not sure why so many more young people are harming themselves than in the past, if indeed they are. According to Joe Ferns, emotional health promotion manager for the Samaritans, 'It's hard to be sure if teenage self-harm really is on the increase or whether we're just more aware of it now, looking for it and asking the right questions so we find it. Some believe that the more you talk about an issue the more acceptable it becomes to come forward and talk about it.

'Young people are certainly under more pressure than in the past, particularly because of the education system, with its emphasis on coursework and targets. Children are having to take more responsibility for their futures from a much younger age. This could explain an increase in self-harm.'

Ferns believes that modern coping strategies – or the lack of them – may also be to blame. 'Whereas in the past we used to rely on support networks, we now tend to cope alone, as individuals, retreating into our rooms, listening to music or escaping through TV. Alone and in pain, a person is more likely to take out their feelings on themself.'

Images of self-harm are all around us, particularly in religious iconography. Christianity is founded on the notion that Christ suffered for the world's sins and there have been sects which practised self-flagellation and mutilation throughout history. Pain and the spilling of our own blood are seen as ways of cleansing ourselves. Likewise, when teenagers cut themselves they often say it is a release, a way of punishing themselves or others.

'The pain proves you're human'

Josephine Lowe (name changed) is 16. She began self-harming at 13. 'I started cutting myself when I could no longer cope with being bullied about my weight and the way I look. It had been going on for 18 months and I was so desperate that the only way out I could see was to commit suicide. But when I tried to slit my wrists I couldn't go through with it. So I cut my arms instead. I was angry at myself and my body and it was a way of punishing myself.

'I felt totally calm and rational when I did it, like I was finally in control of my life. And the whole experience was such a relief. The pain is so intense that it gives you something to focus all your energy on – it helps you prove that you are still human and still have feelings.

'From that point on it became my release. Whenever things got on top of me, when I was angry or upset, I'd go into my bedroom and cut myself. I'd use a knife or razors, whatever was handy. Sometimes I'd just make surface scratches and at other times, cut really deep, depending on how sharp the blade was and how I felt. I'd clean up the blood and hide the cuts and scars under long-sleeved tops.

'It got to the stage where I was harming myself every day and it was completely spinning out of control. It was like an addiction. Every time I cut myself I felt a tremendous buzz, a high. I wanted to keep feeling like that but I also hated myself for doing it. I knew it was dangerous – that I could cut an artery by mistake or get a serious infection. I tried really hard to cover up the marks and made up loads of lies about how I got them, pretending I'd fallen over or that the cat had scratched me.

'Eventually, my dad saw the scars. He got really upset and started hiding the knives and razors and checking my arms every day. I know he was only trying to help but it just made things worse. My lowest point was when people at school found out. It felt like everybody was looking at me and loads of people kept coming up to me and asking why I wanted to slit my wrists.

'In December 2001, when I was 14, I couldn't cope with things any more and took an overdose. Cutting myself was no longer releasing my pain and I just wanted it all to end. I was referred to an adolescent mental health unit for treatment. I still see a psychologist there.

'I haven't self-harmed for several months now and my scars have largely faded. I realised I had to move on and stop being self-destructive. I've just passed my GCSEs and I really want to be a journalist. I'm also planning to set up a bullying helpline next year.'

The difference nowadays is that teenage icons are more likely to be pop stars or celebrities. Before he vanished in February 1995, the Manic Street Preachers' Richie Edwards famously carved the words '4 Real' into his arm as a public expression of his mental torment. Ferns says such images glamorise cutting, romanticising the practice. 'Some self-harm websites actually seem to encourage young people to experiment with self-harm,' he adds.

Ferns also worries about the effect of peer pressure on teenagers. 'Our research shows a high correlation between people who self-harm and family members or friends who engage in the practice. People who have friends who self-harm are more likely to do it themselves.' This suggests that publicity about the practice – even when it is well-meaning, such as a recent storyline in the teenage television soap *Hollyoaks* – might actually be counterproductive.

The general perception is that we live in a more violent, dangerous society than that of the past. But statistics fail to support this impression. Perhaps the truth is rather more disturbing. In modern Britain the only real increase in violence is in that which we inflict on ourselves. If our children do come to harm it is more than likely to be at their own hands.

■ This article first appeared in *The Guardian*, 2 September 2003.

© *Hilary Freeman*

Self-harm: the facts

Information from the Basement Project

People self-harm in different ways

Some cut their arms or legs, others bang or bruise their bodies. Self-harm also includes burning, scratching, hair-pulling, scrubbing, or anything that causes injury to the body. Some people take tablets, perhaps not a big overdose, but enough to blot things out for a while. Some people hurt themselves just once or twice. Other people use self-harm to cope over a long time. They might hurt themselves quite often during a bad patch.

Self-harm isn't necessarily about suicide

Sometimes people harm themselves because they want to die. But often it's more about staying alive. People may hurt themselves to help them get through a bad time. It's a way to cope.

It's not 'just attention-seeking'

People self-harm because they are in pain and trying to cope. They could also be trying to show that something is wrong. They need to be taken seriously.

It doesn't mean you're off your head

All sorts of people self-harm. Even people in high-powered jobs. It's a sign that something is bothering and upsetting you, not that you are mad. You may not have met anyone else who self-harms and may even think you are the only one who

Things like starving, overeating, drinking too much, risk-taking, smoking and many others are also types of 'self-harm'

does it. There's a lot of secrecy about self-harm. But many thousands of people cope in this way for a while.

Other things can be 'self-harm' too

Things like starving, overeating, drinking too much, risk-taking, smoking and many others are also types of 'self-harm'. Some coping methods (like burying yourself in work) may be more acceptable, but can still be harmful.

People do stop self-harming

Many people stop self-harming – when they're ready. They sort their problems out and find other ways of dealing with their feelings. It might take a long time and they might need help. But things can get better.

You can get help

If you are worried about self-harm you can get help. Self-harm is often a way of coping with painful experiences. These might include being abused or neglected, losing someone important to you, being bullied, harassed or assaulted, or being very lonely and isolated. It helps to tell someone supportive about painful things that have happened to you and the ways these have made you feel.

About the Basement Project

Our work is founded on respect for individuals and for their rights to determine their own needs and make choices for themselves. We provide low-cost books on self-harm for those who cope in this way and for workers, families and friends.

© The Basement Project

Injuries

Numbers and types of injuries by gender in NCH projects during a 3-month period

Types of injury	Male Number	%	Female Number	%	Total Number	%
Cutting	34	16	98	32	132	25
Inflicting blows	45	21	31	10	76	15
Burning/scalding	7	3	10	3	17	3
Picking/scratching	41	19	64	21	105	20
Pulling out hair	15	7	26	8	41	8
Biting	27	13	24	8	51	10
Swallowing objects	17	8	19	6	36	7
Inserting objects	4	2	7	2	11	2
Other	24	11	27	9	51	10
Total	214	100	306	100	520	100

Source: 'Look beyond the scars', NCH

Shock figures

Shock figures show as many as two adolescents in every classroom may be self-harming

Government figures suggest that one in seventeen adolescents – nearly two in every classroom – are self-harming. New research, goes behind these horrifying statistics to cast new light on why young people self-harm, and on the help they say they need but often don't receive.

NCH and Coventry University's research found that the onset of self-harm was often linked to difficulties in young people's lives such as being bullied at school, unwanted pregnancy, parental divorce and bereavement. The earliest age of onset of self-harm in the study was seven and although the frequency varied, at its peak, one of the people interviewed had harmed herself over ten times a day, by cutting or blood-letting.

Caroline Abrahams, Director of Public Policy at NCH, said: 'The Government's own research suggests that more than 200,000 11- 15-year-olds are self-harming, but the study we are publishing today shows that behind every one of them is a young person – and often a family – in deep distress.'

Joint author of the report, Professor Paul Bywaters of the Centre for Social Justice at Coventry University, said: 'Everyone who works with children and young people needs to be much more alert to this issue. We must lift the taboo that surrounds self-harm so that children and families get the help they need. Above all, the Government must invest a lot more money in local services for children with problems like self-harm, and their families.'

Alongside the report, NCH is also launching a leaflet and a website – http://www.nch.org.uk/selfharm with advice and information about self-harm for young people, and for their families and friends.

Rather than being a 'near suicide attempt', as most people think it to be, for the people in this study self-harm was more often a way of coping with the pressures of modern living that can take such a toll on children and young people – a way of preventing suicide. They explained that self-harm gave them a sense of release and a means of expressing their distress, even though they usually harmed themselves in private.

Mel (late teens) said: 'When I do it, it feels like one thing that I have control over. It's one thing that I can decide, how hard I hit that wall.'

'We must lift the taboo that surrounds self-harm so that children and families get the help they need'

Tammy (early 20s) said: 'It made the pain go away . . . I wouldn't have to cry and I'd feel happy again . . . '

Another part of the study looked at the incidence of self-harm among children and young people who attend NCH's projects, and found that over 3 in 5 of those responding said at least one incident of self-

harm had occurred in the project during the last three months.

NCH is one of the leading providers of children's services in the UK so this suggests that self-harm is a significant, but often hidden problem in all children's services and one that such agencies need to do more to plan for and take into account.

Self-harm can be very frightening and difficult to deal with, so people who work with children need training and support to help them respond sensitively and well. The young people who took part in the study had very varied experiences of professionals; some were caring and helpful but others were less sympathetic:

Phil (over 25) said: 'One of the sisters in A&E has stood for an hour and a half stitching me up . . . they've never turned round once and said "you're a pain in the arse for keeping coming in. Why do you do it?"'

Anna (late teens) said: 'I think they (hospital staff) think it's a waste of time, because they should be treating people who don't hurt themselves rather than having to treat people who do.'

Note

The summary and leaflet can both be seen and downloaded by visiting http://www.nch.org.uk

The research was carried out for NCH by Professor Paul Bywaters and Alison Rolfe at the Centre for Social Justice at Coventry University. The method was a survey of NCH projects across England, Wales and Scotland and confidential interviews with 19 service users who have self-harmed and 5 people who were their friends or partners, during 2000 and 2001.

■ The above information is from NCH's web site which can be found at www.nch.org.uk Alternatively see their address details on page 41.

© NCH

Self-harm

Information from the Mental Health Foundation

What is self-harm?

Self-harm is causing deliberate hurt to your own body, most commonly by cutting, but also by burning, abusing drugs, alcohol or other substances. This occurs at times of extreme anger, distress and low self-esteem, in order to either create a physical manifestation of the negative feelings which can then be dealt with, or alternatively to punish yourself. Sometimes linked with hearing voices – particularly as a way of stopping the voices.

How many people are affected?

Like anorexia it has a higher prevalence in teenagers and young people. Also like anorexia it is more commonly experienced by women than by men. The best estimate is 1 in 130 people – 446,000 or nearly half a million across the UK.

The only recorded figures are from hospital admissions to Accident & Emergency (A&E) (142,000 resulting hospital admissions per year in England and Wales), but the numbers of people who self-harm who refer or are referred to A&E will be very small. This is because self-harm itself is not an attempt at fatal injury, but rather an attempt to inflict harm without the need for medical intervention. Most people who self-harm will make every effort to ensure that they stay out of A&E – largely because of the unsympathetic response that they expect there.

Is it a growing issue?

The issue is becoming more widely recognised. But it's difficult to say whether the numbers of people self-harming are themselves increasing. It is much more common than could be seen from the only available statistics but it is very probable that there have been high numbers for a long time – it's not something that's suddenly started happening. What's changing is the increasing willingness on the part of service users to talk

about the issue and their dissatisfaction with services.

Myths

Attention seeking

People who self-harm tend to do so in private. They often do not tell friends, colleagues or family of what is happening. Because of the stigma and low self-esteem they are unlikely to seek help.

It doesn't hurt

Of course it hurts. The initial sensation may be blunted by the intensity of emotion but yes, if you cut yourself deeply it will hurt.

Typical background/ history

The use of self-harming as a coping or self-management strategy could be seen as similar to the control that people with anorexia feel over their bodies. Self-harming, similar to anorexia, can become habitual – specifically at particular points of a regular cycle of mental distress – and, again like anorexia, it is usually only a visible condition when extreme.

Self-harm is often associated with depression, low self-esteem and a poor physical self-image. There is also a strong association with sexual

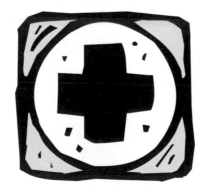

abuse. People who self-harm will often start doing so at the age of 14 or 15, although many continue to do so for many years.

How can self-harm be prevented?

People who self-harm find a variety of personal strategies useful to minimise or manage their approach including:

- Having a better understanding of why and when you self-harm – and identifying those people who are supportive and make you feel good about yourself – building up your support network.
- Minimisation – making a small cut rather than a big one, using clean implements. This may mean cutting earlier rather than later when the distress has built up.
- Distraction – trying to go and do something else rather than cut yourself.
- Avoidance – not keeping razor blades or other sharp objects in the house.
- Deterrent – having the item with which you self-harm in sight all the time as a reminder not to use it.
- Talking – talk to somebody whom you see as 'safe'.

Anybody who is concerned about somebody who is self-harming should be aware that they cannot necessarily change their friend or relative's life or coping mechanisms. Instead they should simply try to be caring, respectful and willing to listen (if that is what is wanted) while allowing their friend or relative to retain their dignity. They should not patronise, condemn, judge, attempt to explain or control, or panic (however hard this may seem!).

■ The above information is from the Mental Health Foundation's web site which can be found at www.mentalhealth.org.uk

© *Mental Health Foundation*

Myth breaking

For family and friends who have never self-harmed being faced with this is a daunting task which they often feel there is no guide for. This is why people often make incorrect assumptions

'Self-harm is a suicide attempt'
Self-harm is not the same as suicide. Somebody who tries to commit suicide feels they have no option and no way out of their pain. However, a person who is self-harming is surviving in the best way possible for them at this time. Some people who do self-harm can become suicidal if they are also depressed and if they feel self-harm is no longer working for them.

'Self-harm means borderline personality disorder'
A borderline personality disorder requires 9 criteria one of which is self-harm. However, often doctors can diagnose a person as borderline personality disordered at first knowledge of self-harm. This is because self harm itself is not seen as a separate illness so doctors feel the need to catorogise it.

'Self-harm means sexual abuse'
Many people who self-harm have experienced some form of sexual abuse; however, it does not follow that if someone is self-harming they must have been sexually abused. Often self-harmers who have had no previous abuse are concerned about the impact of people's assumptions of abuse when self-harm is disclosed.

'Mad/crazy/schizophrenic/ psychotic people self-harm'
Most people who self-harm do not have a serious mental illness. They are struggling with problems such as depression, anxiety and eating disorders which are treatable. People who self-harm are not mad or crazy, they just are in great emotional pain.

'She/he has been self-harming for years, they are beyond help'
No person is beyond help. Everybody can live without self-harm if they have access to the right kind of support.

'If self-harm does not require stitches or is only superficial it is not serious'
All self-harm is serious. If you discover someone is self-harming it means they have intense emotional pain and the level/severity of their wounds are irrelevant to this pain. Also the self-harm you may be seeing may only be a small part of the person's current self-harm injuries.

'Self-harm means a danger to others'
People who self-harm are highly unlikely to hurt others. This is because they are turning their pain in on themselves instead of directing it at others.

'Self-harm is attention seeking'
Most people who self-harm do not do so for attention. If that was their purpose there are much easier, less painful, ways of achieving this. The

---

Everybody can live without self-harm if they have access to the right kind of support

---

Self Harm Alliance likes to say they are seeking care. They are calling out via unspoken communication to ask for love, understanding, support, acceptance and kindness.

'Self-harm is related to sexual masochism'
A person who self-harms is not the same as someone who has sexual behaviours and fantasies involving the real act of being humiliated, bound or otherwise made to suffer.

Self-harm is Munchausen's syndrome'
Munchausen's syndrome is where a person becomes obsessed about being unwell and will present physical symptoms such as sickness, diarrhoea, fevers etc. A person who self-harms does not have Munchausen's syndrome, the self-harm is caused by real intense emotional pain. The self-harmer often does not go out of their way to seek medical care for the self-harm and often keeps it a secret from many people.

■ The above information is from the Self Harm Alliance's web site: www.selfharmalliance.org Alternatively, see page 41 for their address details.

© Self Harm Alliance

Women and self-injury

Information from the Bristol Crisis Service for Women

What is self-injury?

'Self-injury' is any sort of self-harm which involves inflicting injuries or pain on one's own body. It can take many forms.

The most common form of self-injury is probably cutting, usually superficially, but sometimes deeply. Women may also burn themselves, punch themselves or hit their bodies against something. Some people pick their skin or pull out hair.

How common is self-injury?

Self-injury is far more widespread than is generally realised. All sorts of people self-injure. Often they carry on successful careers or look after families and there is little outward sign that there is anything wrong. Self-injury seems to be more common among women, partly because men are more likely to express strong feelings such as anger outwardly.

Many women who self-injure believe they are the only person that hurts themselves in this way. Fear and shame may force women to keep self-injury secret for many years. This means that the true extent of the problem is unknown. Our experience shows that where it is acceptable to talk about, many women reveal that they have self-injured at some time.

Why do women self-injure?

There are always powerful reasons why a woman hurts herself. For most women it is a way of surviving great emotional pain.

Many people cope with difficulties in their lives in ways which are risky and harmful to themselves. Some drink or eat too much, smoke, drive too fast, gamble or make themselves ill through overwork or worry. They might do this to numb or distract themselves from problems or feelings they cannot bear to face (like 'drowning your sorrows').

Self-injury, though more shocking, bears many similarities to these 'ordinary' forms of self-harm. Like drink or drugs, hurting herself may help a woman block out painful feelings. Like taking risks or gambling, it may provide danger and distraction.

Often women say that self-injury helps them to release unbearable tension, which may arise from anxiety, grief or anger. It puts their pain outside, where it feels easier to cope with. For others it relieves feelings of guilt or shame. Sometimes a woman's self-injury is a 'cry for help'; a way of showing (even to herself) that she has suffered and is in pain. Perhaps hurting herself is a way of feeling 'real' and alive, or having control over something in her life. What lies behind women's distress may be painful experiences in childhood or adulthood. A woman may have suffered neglect or abuse, or may have always been criticised or silenced, rather than supported and allowed to express her needs and feelings. Some women who self-injure lost parents early, or came from chaotic or violent families. For others, adult experiences of emotional or physical cruelty have led to their desperation.

Myths about self-injury

Self-injury is a failed suicide attempt

Self-injury is a way of carrying on with life, not of dying. Injuries are seldom life-threatening. It is important to distinguish self-injury from a suicide attempt, so that its true meanings can be understood.

Self-injury is 'just attention seeking'

Self-injury is primarily about helping oneself cope with great pain. For some,

it is a desperate attempt to show that something is really wrong, and attention should be paid to their distress.

Self-injury is a sign of madness
Self-injury is a sign of distress, not madness; a sign of someone trying to cope with her life as best she can.

A person who self-injures is a danger to others
Someone who self-injures is directing her hurt and anger at herself, not at others. Most would be appalled at the idea of hurting someone else.

What can help?
Self-injury causes great distress, and can seem a difficult problem to overcome. But it is possible for a woman to stop hurting herself, if she can understand and resolve the problems behind what she does.

If you are someone who self-injures
Think about what your self-injury is 'saying' about your feelings and your life. This will give you clues about problems you need to work on. You might find it helpful to talk about your self-injury and what lies behind it with friends or a counsellor. To find out about counselling, you could ask your GP, Women's Centre, rape or sexual abuse support service, MIND group, library, Wellwoman clinic, or Citizens' Advice Bureau.

If you want to help someone who self-injures
Naturally you may feel upset, shocked or angry when someone you care about hurts herself. Try to keep seeing the person in pain behind the injuries. The most precious things you can offer are acceptance and support. Let your friend know you understand that self-injury is helping her to cope at the moment. She is not 'bad' or 'mad' for doing it. You could invite her to talk about her feelings, or to call you if she is having a difficult time. But only offer as much as you can cope with, and don't try to take responsibility for stopping her from hurting herself.

• Bristol Crisis Service for Women is a charity set up in 1986 to respond to the needs of women in emotional distress. We have a focus on self-injury and have carried out extensive research. We also provide information and publications, and training for professionals. UK National Helpline for women in distress Friday and Saturday nights 9pm to 12.30am and Sunday 6-9pm 0117 925 1119. We offer any woman who rings a chance to talk through her feelings in confidence, without fear of being judged or dismissed. Around half our calls relate to self injury.

The helpline is also available to young women and we have published a self-help journal for young people who self-injure.

■ The above information is from Bristol Crisis Service for Women. Visit their web site at www.users.zetnet.co.uk/bcsw
© Bristol Crisis Service for Women

Self-harm

Why are so many women hurting themselves?

By Beverley Kemp

About 1.5 million people in the UK deliberately inflict some form of injury on themselves every year – with 10,000 needing hospital treatment – and increasing numbers are mutilating their own bodies as a way of releasing emotional pain. Disturbingly, the majority are women.

'One stereotype of the woman who self-harms is that she is mentally ill,' says Dr Rory O'Connor, head of the Suicidal Behaviour Research Group at the University of Strathclyde. 'The reality is that she's more likely to be an average person who's undergone a lot of emotional stress and is having trouble coping.' Kirsti Reeve, 33, a PhD student who cut herself from the age of 19 to 29, now runs a web site called www.self-injury.info that offers support to self-harmers. Her site receives over 200 hits daily and the youngest visitors are girls of 12. Research shows that self-harm tends to start in adolescence, although adult trauma can also precipitate it. Princess Diana is alleged to have scratched her wrists and tried to throw herself down a flight of stairs as a result of emotional distress.

All cut up
So what exactly is self-harm and why are more women doing it? Self-harming is the deliberate causing of pain and injuries to your own body. The most common method is cutting. A 1995 survey of 76 women aged 118 to their late 50s, carried out by Lois Arnold for the Bristol Crisis Service for Women, revealed that 90 per cent cut themselves using razor blades, knives or broken glass. Most hurt their arms or hands, but a significant proportion cut their legs, face, stomach, breasts or genitals.

Other forms of self-injury include burning, punching, and head-banging. Extreme examples include pulling out hair, biting themselves and swallowing harmful substances and objects.

'Most people self-harm in some way, although they might not recognise it. Perhaps they smoke, drink heavily, or work too hard,' says Hilary Lindsay, co-ordinator of the Bristol Crisis Service for Women. 'Others stay in abusive or unfulfilling relationships.' Further examples include over-exercising, compulsive spending, eating disorders and committing petty crimes. 'The reasons people self-injure vary,' says Lindsay, 'but most people do so because they've found it relieves them of unbearable feelings. Some women say that, for them, physical pain is much easier to handle than emotional pain. Others need to see blood flowing to feel release from deep emotional hurt.'

Inner turmoil

It's a behaviour pattern that Kirsti Reeve knows only too well. 'I used to feel emotions building up inside me – and cutting myself felt as if I was releasing the value on a pressure cooker,' she says. 'The moment that I saw the blood, I experienced a tremendous sense of relief and was able to relax. It was also a reminder that I was alive.'

'Some people say that, for them, physical pain is much easier to handle than emotional pain'

While some women describe their first experience of self-injury as instinctive behaviour that quickly becomes habitual, for others it's a one-off response to internal turmoil. Jo Smith,* 26, cut her arms for a six-month period during her teens when her mother was diagnosed with clinical depression. 'Looking back,' she says, 'I think it was my way of saying, "Listen to me" because my mother's illness made me feel abandoned and helpless. When she got better, I had no desire to do it again.' Jan Sutton, counsellor and author of *Healing the Hurt Within* (Pathways, £12.95), says that 'A minority of young people may experiment once or twice to mimic their peers or "fit in" but repetitive acts of self-harm normally point to an underlying problem, such as low self-esteem, family problems, exam stress, bullying, abuse, rape, lack of emotional support or bereavement.'

Neglect and abuse

'Current research into self-injury suggests that women do it more than men,' says Sutton. 'This may be because one of the key functions of self-injury is to release suppressed anger. Society is more inclined to tolerate displays of aggression from males (such as fights or competitive sports) and so men tend to channel their anger outwards, whereas women are more likely to internalise it. However, it's also possible that men may be more reluctant to admit that they self-harm due to the "big boys don't cry" syndrome.'

Another explanation for why more women than men self-harm is that a higher percentage have experienced one of the main factors that research shows can trigger self-harming tendencies. The Bristol Crisis Service for Women survey revealed that 49 per cent of respondents had experienced neglect or sexual abuse as a child. Forty-three per cent had suffered emotional abuse and 25 per cent physical abuse as children. However, it must be stressed that, while some women who self-injure come from chaotic or violent family situations, many others do not. What may not be a particularly stressful event for one person can have a huge impact on another, and their ability to cope depends on their support networks. 'One of the key factors in the psychological profile of self-harmers is isolation and feelings of trauma that they can't escape from,' says Dr O'Connor.

Self-mutilation may be reported more openly than ever before, but for many it's still a taboo. 'It's not a comfortable subject to talk about because it arouses strong emotions in others – shock, horror, sadness, guilt and fear,' says Sutton. She believes that raised awareness may have given young women permission to come out of the closet and ask for help. However, Dr O'Connor has evidence that it can also lead to copycat incidents. 'There have been examples where the leader of a group of teenage girls starts self-injuring and the others follow as they think it's a cool thing to do,' he says. The celebrity-obsessed climate we lie in may also have a part to play. 'It can make younger women feel pressurised to be thin, beautiful and have an attractive partner,' he says. 'Feeling that you fall short can lead to psychological pain. Self-harming is the outcome of internal trauma, and the most important thing is to treat the cause. Therapy and counselling can help by encouraging an individual to explore painful issues from their past and discover various different strategies to deal with emotional stress.'

Self-help

Sutton points out that self-harm has

Self-harm has an addictive quality about it and that there is no magic cure

an addictive quality about it and that there is no magic cure. In her book, the self-harmers she interviewed suggested a wide range of self-help strategies, including releasing feelings through writing poetry or keeping a journal, using a helpline or talking things through with a trusted friend or family member, constructive expressions of anger, such as pounding cushions or taking a martial-arts course, repeating positive statements such as, 'I am a worthwhile person' and learning stress-management and relaxation techniques. Reeve says she found therapy useful but also employed substitute behaviours. 'I cut because I needed to see blood, so I painted my nails red and dyed my hair red so I could see the colour flow down the sink. I know women who put red food colouring in ice cubes so they can hold them in their hands and see them melt. It gives release without actually hurting yourself.' Reeve says that one of the most supportive things you can do if a loved one is self-injuring is not to judge them and to try to understand that they're doing it because they're hurting inside. 'Self-harmers feel enough shame without people adding to it,' she says. 'Instead, try to encourage them to find a form of help they feel comfortable with. Realising they are not alone is an important first step.'

■ Contact the Bristol Crisis Service for Women helpline on 0117 9251119 (Friday and Saturday evenings, 9pm to 12.30am; Sundays, 6pm to 9pm).

■ For more information on self-harm, visit the SIARI (Self-Injury and Related Issues) web site at www.siari.co.uk

* Name has been changed,

■ The above article appeared in *Zest* magazine, February 2003. Visit their web site at www.zest.co.uk

© *National Magazine Company Limited*

Guiding light

By Polly Curtis

In December 2002, Universities UK published guidelines on how to prevent suicides among students, following research that showed about 40% of undergraduates will be troubled by mental health difficulties.

Each year, many students decide to end their lives, despite living in what is considered a recognised community. In 1997 to 1998, the last year for which there is available data, there were 178 suicides or undetermined deaths among students.

Although recent research has shown that the suicide rate among students is not greater than that of the general population, their mental health is significantly poorer, and many believe it is getting worse.

UUK, which represents university vice-chancellors, believes more could be done to prevent student suicides. The wording in its guidelines is careful; there are strategies to attempt to reduce the risk of suicide, but it could be impossible to prevent every suicide.

The guidelines were written by Annie Grant, from the educational development and support centre at the University of Leicester, with the help of student counsellors, university support services and mental health charities. Ms Grant says staff and students need to be on the lookout for signs of mental distress.

'At Leicester we produced guidance for staff on students who are distressed. Students don't always go to support staff. Academic staff need to know what the signs and symptoms are. Student services need to be strengthened, but because we know suicidal students don't seek help it's crucially important that staff are trained to be aware of the signs,' she says.

Staff at Leicester have been issued with information helping

In 1997 to 1998, the last year for which there is available data, there were 178 suicides or undetermined deaths among students

---

them to recognise a problem with a student.

But, says Ms Grant, it's a job for the whole community. 'Other students can also, in the same way, be aware. The sources of help that students are most likely to seek are family and friends in the university. We need to educate the whole student body about the signs of distress. They are often the ones who are alerting universities.'

Information posters have been placed in all of Leicester's accommodation common rooms.

But what can a student do if they are worried for a friend or flatmate? 'Confidentiality is hugely important. But if there is a risk of harm, it's worth breaking that confidentiality,' says Ms Grant. 'We have trained sub-wardens in the halls, or you could go to a personal tutor. Very often it's when you start putting the picture together you start understanding more. Have they been handing their essays in? They can talk in confidence to tutors or the counselling services. It's important that they do mention it to someone. If they talk to student services, they

---

Sources of help following suicide attempts

About half (52%) of respondents who had ever attempted suicide, said they had sought some help.

By sex

Source of help*	Men	Women	Total
Friend/family/neighbours	22%	27%	25%
GP	26%	25%	25%
Specialist medical service	25%	33%	30%
Voluntary service	3%	2%	2%
Someone else	3%	1%	2%
Received help	48%	54%	52%
Did not receive help	52%	46%	48%
Base (= Respondents who had attempted suicide)	156	273	429

By age

Source of help*	16-24	25-44	45-64	65-74	Total
Friend/family/neighbours	40%	22%	20%	[5%]	25%
GP	21%	26%	28%	[5%]	25%
Specialist medical service	18%	33%	28%	[13%]	30%
Voluntary service	-	3%	3%	[0%]	2%
Someone else	1%	3%	-	[0%]	2%
Received help	51%	52%	52%	[14%]	52%
Did not receive help	49%	48%	48%	[10%]	48%
Base (= Respondents who had attempted suicide)	48	231	126	24	429

* Percentages sum to more than the 'Received help' total as respondents could give more than one answer

Source: Crown copyright

will help guide them to their next course of action. The thing to do is not ignore it.'

The work at Leicester, which was co-developed by the University of Nottingham, has been adopted elsewhere, but it is an ongoing process. Every time a student anywhere commits suicide, universities across Britain re-examine what they are doing, says Ms Grant.

Verity Coyle, welfare officer at the National Union of Students, said things are beginning to change. 'There are obviously gaps in the support system at the moment, and there needs to be more pre-emptive work done. But there's been more encouragement and community spirit at universities recently and help is becoming accessible,' she said.

Sophie Allchin is co-ordinator of London University Nightline, a telephone counselling service run for and by students. Similar services can be found in 50 universities around the country. Nightline was first set up at Imperial College in London after several students committed suicide in 1971. Ms Allchin says the call centre usually deals with students with relationship difficulties or depression.

'I think it is a massive shock for students going to university, particularly in London where it is so isolated. You're not on a campus, there are increasing financial pressures and people feeling they are the only ones without friends. Often people don't want to worry or disappoint friends and family,' says Ms Allchin.

But she adds: 'There are welfare officers at most student unions, counselling services, personal tutors and wardens in halls. There are enough services, but I don't know whether people hear about it enough. Getting people to seek help can be impossible.'

Identifying difficulties

The first time academic staff become aware that a student is experiencing difficulties may be when he or she is persistently absent from lectures or classes, fails to meet course deadlines or when coursework marks drop dramatically. Sometimes a student's problems may lead to them doing too much work, rather than too little. Other signs include:

- behaviour that indicates a student is persistently tense, sad or miserable
- loud, agitated or aggressive behaviour
- very withdrawn or unusually quiet behaviour
- erratic or unpredictable behaviour
- unkempt personal appearance, significant weight changes or decline in personal hygiene

If concern is expressed, some students may readily open up and discuss the problem. However, others may conceal their difficulties so successfully the nature of their problems cannot easily be detected. A student may also feel embarrassed or concerned about the consequences of telling someone in their department, or hope the problem will go away.

Source: University of Leicester, *Helping students in difficulty*
© *Guardian Newspapers Limited 2003*

Suicide prevention strategy

Strategy seeks to cut number of suicides by 20% in eight years. By John Carvel, Social Affairs Editor

The first national suicide prevention strategy was launched by ministers in September 2002 in an attempt to reduce the number of people taking their lives by at least 20% within eight years.

It will target young men, prisoners, farmers, and other high risk groups in England, to identify better ways of providing mental health services to the people who need them most.

A cross-government network will be set up to look at how factors such as unemployment and poor housing can have a particularly severe impact on people with mental health problems.

Local authorities will be asked to improve safety at suicide hotspots such as cliffs and railway bridges.

Jacqui Smith, the health minister, said that £329m was set aside in the NHS plan to improve community mental health services, including the provision of more crisis resolution teams.

'Suicide is devastating and on average a person dies every two hours as a result of it . . . each suicide represents an individual tragedy and a loss to society,' she said.

About 5,000 people commit suicide in England each year. It is the commonest cause of death in men under 35 and the main cause of premature death among people with mental illness. The strategy's goals include:

- to reduce risk among groups such as men under 35, with measures including national monitoring of non-fatal incidents of deliberate self-harm;
- to reduce the availability and effectiveness of suicidal methods, including safer prescribing of antidepressants;
- to improve the reporting in the media of suicidal behaviour;
- to improve monitoring of suicide rates by age, gender, methods used, and victims' use of mental health services.

Mind, the mental health charity, said the strategy was good, but the government was undermining it by bringing forward plans for mental health legislation that would deter people from seeking help if they got depressed.

The suicide strategy came as the government finished consulting on reform of the Mental Health Act. An alliance of 50 mental health charities delivered a giant letter to the Department of Health in London warning against plans for compulsory detention and treatment of people with dangerous personality disorder.

© *Guardian Newspapers Limited 2003*

Stigma ties

Can changes in public policy have an impact on reducing suicides in Britain?

By Angela Lambert

Suicides in Britain are far more numerous than deaths caused by traffic accidents. 'Not quite twice as many, but about 70% more – and that always makes people sit up,' says Keith Hawton, professor of psychiatry and director of the centre for suicide research at the Warneford hospital in Oxford.

Manic depression, mental illness and the suicide that often results are a major problem worldwide. According to the World Health Organisation, by 2020 about 1.5m people a year are likely to kill themselves. Globally, suicide is already among the top 10 causes of death and is one of three leading causes in the 15-34 age group. In England, it is the commonest cause among men under 35.

Starting next weekend, the biennial European symposium on suicide and suicidal behaviour is being held for the first time in England, at Warwick University, jointly organised by Hawton's research centre and the Samaritans. It will take place over four days, during which 400 delegates will give hundreds of papers on topics ranging from 'Making sense of railway suicide' to 'The impact of gun control on suicide in Canada'.

The title of this, the ninth, symposium is 'From Science to Practice'. The crucial point is not just to investigate, but to act on the results. Speakers are being encouraged to interpret their findings in the light of clinical practice and public health strategies. Simon Armson, chief executive of the Samaritans, says: 'There's a huge amount going on in trying to understand the phenomenon of suicide, but it has to be applied in practice. We're bringing together the most up-to-date thinking for discussion, sharing, and implementing.'

But can public policy have any effect on the private hell of manic depression that drives people to suicide? 'Public policy tends to drive public opinion, which at its worst expresses stigma and taboo, so by changing policy you also affect public opinion,' argues Armson. 'A great deal can be done to influence the way manic depression and suicide are experienced and endured. Those afflicted have enough to contend with, without the extra burden of seeming to be mad and therefore being shunned.

'Until quite recently, suicide was illegal – the very use of the expression "to commit" suicide implies that it's a crime. We need to use other – and I don't mean politically correct – phrases, like "dying by suicide", or "killing yourself" or "taking your own life", to remove that taint of criminality. Suicides used not to be buried in consecrated ground – now they are treated just like anyone else who has died. We have to encourage people to see manic depression as being just as much an illness as appendicitis. Stigmatising something or someone is often a way of failing to recognise your own particular difficulties and concerns. When people are afraid, they resort to

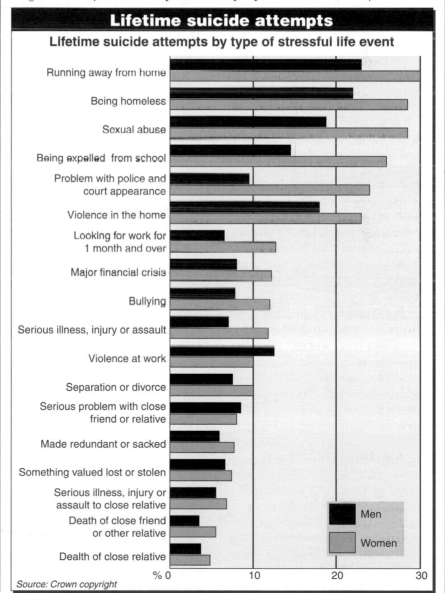

Lifetime suicide attempts

Lifetime suicide attempts by type of stressful life event

- Running away from home
- Being homeless
- Sexual abuse
- Being expelled from school
- Problem with police and court appearance
- Violence in the home
- Looking for work for 1 month and over
- Major financial crisis
- Bullying
- Serious illness, injury or assault
- Violence at work
- Separation or divorce
- Serious problem with close friend or relative
- Made redundant or sacked
- Something valued lost or stolen
- Serious illness, injury or assault to close relative
- Death of close friend or other relative
- Death of close relative

Men
Women

% 0   10   20   30

Source: Crown copyright

ridicule. The more people know about mental illness, the less it will be sidelined and regarded as a shameful secret,' says Armson.

The government agrees. Its current target is a 20% reduction in the number of suicides by 2010. Health minister Jacqui Smith is expected to launch a national suicide prevention strategy at the symposium, following a three-month consultation earlier this year. In practical terms, the government can support research aimed at suicide prevention. It can improve services for people with mental health problems. And it can discourage the media from giving over-dramatic accounts of suicides, since it has been proved that this can lead to a rise in the number of similar suicides. A rather dramatic paracetamol overdose in an episode of *Casualty*, the BBC hospital drama, is considered to have led to an increase in paracetamol suicides in the following weeks – clear evidence, says Hawton, of a copycat effect.

The government could also put more effort into preventing suicide; for example, by reducing the methods available. When non-toxic North Sea gas was first introduced, people could no longer die by gassing themselves. This probably saved about 6,000 lives. When the numbers of paracetamol tablets in a packet was set at a maximum of 12, there was a dramatic reduction in suicides from overdoses of the painkiller.

A guest speaker at the symposium will be Kay Redfield Jamison, professor of psychiatry at the Johns Hopkins University school of medicine in the US and author of *An Unquiet Mind*, a transfixing account of her own manic depression. She speaks from experience. 'There is still a pervasive, insidious and damaging attitude that mental illness is somehow voluntary,' she says. 'Much of it has to do with the possibility of treatment and cure. Before cancer or epilepsy could be treated, there was far more stigma. Effective research and treatment are among the main things in reducing the stigma of mental illness, but we have a long way to go in getting the message out.

'A phrase that drives me mad when people talk about suicide

attempts, is: "She (it's always she) did a very silly thing." That sort of attitude becomes part and parcel of the language. You change it with science – and I'm absolutely convinced science will win the day. We know now that the brain is an organ; not subject to demons or magic, but liable to go wrong like any other organ.'

Armson concurs: 'The difficulties that people with mental illness, or those who have attempted suicide, have in their daily lives are simply not understood. That failure to understand can result in their being shunned or told to "snap out of it" because their behaviour does not conform with what is regarded as normal.' In other words, they are either blamed for not coping, or regarded as mad.

People in acute mental distress go through a period of maximum suicide risk, but it is often quite short-lived. Hawton points out that only a minority who attempt suicide and are saved will actually try again and die. 'A follow-up study of a large group of people who had jumped under tube trains and survived found that, 10 years later, fewer than 10% had gone on to kill themselves,' he says. 'A study of people who were stopped from jumping off the Golden

---

Only a minority who attempt suicide and are saved will actually try again and die

---

Gate Bridge in San Francisco came up with similar results.'

That period of maximum risk can be predicted. Redfield Jamison says: 'The age at which people are most likely to develop mental illness is the late teens. They go off to university, a very vulnerable setting, and start doing the two things most likely to precipitate an episode – drinking, and changing their sleep patterns. The average age of onset for manic depression is 17; for schizophrenia, it's 18-19. This means that the most intensive care should be geared at the early onset of the illness because that's when suicide is most likely to occur.

'The suicide risk for manic depressive people under 30 is 80 times higher than in the general population for a man, and 70-75 times higher for a woman. Drug abuse starts at about the same time, so you need campaigns geared to schools, universities, parents and paediatricians.'

The problems are not intractable. Hawton says the Warwick symposium aims to highlight the best research and to make sure people know about it. 'Suicide is rarely inevitable,' he says. 'After being treated for depression, people often change their view of the world. In his memoir, *Savage God*, Al Alvarez gives a wonderful account of his own suicide attempt with barbiturates. When it failed, he thought, "Well, I'm meant for living; might as well get on with it".'

■ This article first appeared in *The Guardian*, September 2002.

© Angela Lambert

Living on the edge

Information from the Department of Health

Faced with the final straw

Many people contemplating suicide have more than one problem to deal with and then something becomes the final straw.

Volunteer Dave Kerry, who has worked for the Samaritans for 20 years, has spoken to scores close to suicide.

Dave, who lives in Cumbria, is one of more than 18,000 volunteers who between them handled nearly four million calls in England last year, involving 2.2 million hours of listening.

A manager for British Nuclear Fuels at Sellafield, Dave says any phone call can bring a harrowing tale.

Isolated

'I spoke to a young man who was threatening to jump from a high building there and then,' he said. 'He had no relationships in his life. He was alone and isolated.

'Sometimes there is a single factor in a person's life that is the cause. But there are often several and something just becomes the final straw. I have heard a lot of grown men cry over the phone.'

The Samaritans, whose funding includes a contribution from the Department of Health, has been closely involved in the preparation of the National Suicide Prevention Strategy, and the organisation will play a significant role in achieving its objectives.

For example, it has advised local authorities on ways to improve safety at railway 'hotspots' and at bridges and local high places. Its helpline number is on many bridges.

The Samaritans is only too aware of the importance of making access to suicide methods difficult, one of the strategy's key goals. Both the volunteers and the Department of Health know too that improving the well-being of the community as a whole will help reduce suicide.

> **'I spoke to a young man who was threatening to jump from a high building there and then'**

Self-esteem

The strategy stresses the importance of tackling experiences that damage people's self-esteem and social relationships – for example, bullying, low achievement, racial discrimination, family conflict, isolation, violence and abuse.

One of the biggest problems, according to Dave, is dealing with loss – bereavement of a partner after a long life together, the failure of a relationship among young people or a marriage separation.

A caller to the Samaritans from Oxfordshire, a 49-year-old man, explained. 'Everything had come to a head. I was separating from my wife after 13 years. She was moving away with the children and I'd just become redundant.'

Thankfully, he didn't commit suicide. Nor did the young man threatening to jump. The strategy aims to help them if they ever feel like that again.

■ The above article is from the Department of Health's web site which can be found at www.doh.gov.uk

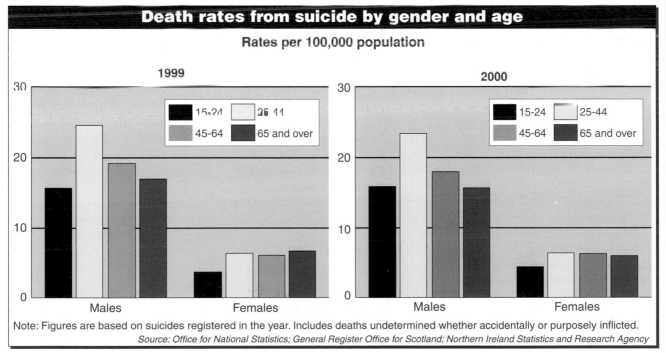

Death rates from suicide by gender and age

Rates per 100,000 population

1999 — Legend: 15-24, 25-44, 45-64, 65 and over — Males, Females

2000 — Legend: 15-24, 25-44, 45-64, 65 and over — Males, Females

Note: Figures are based on suicides registered in the year. Includes deaths undetermined whether accidentally or purposely inflicted.

Source: Office for National Statistics; General Register Office for Scotland; Northern Ireland Statistics and Research Agency

First suicide prevention strategy launched

Scotland's first national suicide prevention strategy which aims to tackle the rising rate of suicides by achieving a 20 per cent reduction in the suicide rate by 2013 was officially launched today.

Choose Life, Preventing Suicide in Scotland: A National Strategy and Action Plan announces new investment of £12 million over the next three years to support national and local action.

Of the total, £9 million is committed for supporting local joint working and training and encouraging local innovation at community level with, at national level, £3 million to support and oversee implementation of the strategy.

In Scotland there were 887 suicides in 2001 – a 22 per cent increase over the last 20 years.

The rate of increase is one of the highest in Europe. The rate for males is almost three times that for females. For young females, the number of those in their early teens being treated for self-harm is also a cause for concern.

Health Minister Malcolm Chisholm said: 'Suicide touches the lives of many people and is a devastating event. It affects all age groups and communities in Scotland. The emotional, social and practical repercussions of suicide are far reaching, felt by family members, friends, colleagues, neighbours and by people working in services.

'Preventing suicide and reducing the rate of suicide in Scotland is an urgent public health issue. It goes right to the heart of our effort and policies to create a healthy, socially inclusive Scotland.

'If we tackle suicide as a "one issue" policy we will fail. In addressing this very serious issue we will work collectively across the Executive – be it economic, social justice, inequality, health, local government, policies for children and young

people, for better public services or for improved mental health.

'Much good work is already being done throughout Scotland. This work must continue but we need to achieve more. Reducing the rate of suicide is not something we can change overnight. This is a long-term strategy with collective responsibility and action.'

The priority groups who should benefit particularly from the strategy are children, young people, people with mental health problems, people who attempt suicide, people affected by suicidal behaviour, those who abuse substances and people in prison.

Seven clear objectives are outlined by the strategy for national and local action on:

- Early Prevention and Intervention: providing earlier intervention and support to prevent problems and reduce the risks that might lead to suicidal behaviour
- Responding to Immediate Crisis: providing support and services to people at risk and people in crisis, to provide an immediate crisis response and to help reduce the severity of any immediate problem
- Longer-term Work to Provide Hope and Support Recovery: providing ongoing support services to enable people to recover and deal with the issues that may be contributing to their suicidal behaviour
- Coping with Suicidal Behaviour and Completed Suicide: providing effective support to those who are affected by suicidal behaviour or a completed suicide
- Promoting Greater Public Awareness and Encouraging People to Seek Help Early: ensuring greater public awareness of positive mental health and well-being, suicidal behaviour, potential problems and risks amongst all age groups and encouraging people to seek help early
- Supporting the Media: ensuring that any depiction of reporting by all sections of the media of a completed suicide or suicidal behaviour is undertaken sensitively and appropriately and with due respect for confidentiality
- Knowing What Works: improving the quality, collection, availability and dissemination of information on issues relating to

suicidal behaviour (and self-harm) and on effective interventions to ensure the better design and implementation of responses and services and use of resources

The strategy will also be supported by a new web-based public mental health resource service which will provide information on suicide, suicidal behaviour and effective intervention to those working in the field of suicide prevention.

A number of milestones are to be placed, marking the progress of the plan towards its target. Progress will be also closely monitored by the strategy National Implementation

Support team through the General Registrar Office Scotland statistics and through the public mental health indicators being developed by the Public Health Institute Scotland (PHIS).

The General Registrar Office figures for suicide and undetermined deaths in Scotland show in 2001: 887 total; 241 female, 646 male (27.1 per cent female, 72.8 per cent male), giving a rate of 9.2 and 26.5 per 100,000 population respectively. (By convention undetermined deaths are included with those from suicide when presenting these figures.)

The Scottish Executive supports the see me campaign addressing the stigma and discrimination which is often associated with mental ill-health.

If a friend is suicidal

People think about killing themselves for lots of reasons. How can you help them to choose to live?

Sometimes just being there and showing that you care is enough to change someone's mind about taking their own life. Occasionally, very sensitive people feel that they don't want to be part of an uncaring world. Looking at the daily news can make death seem attractive if the people around you don't seem too concerned about what happens to others.

From time to time, someone becomes mentally ill. There are several mental illnesses which may cause someone to consider suicide. Depression is very common, about 1 in 4 people may become clinically depressed at some point. It's not just feeling blue, it's much more than that, it's an illness and it can be treated. Some people who are depressed may have to take medicine, others may need to have another type of therapy. A friend can help by understanding something about the illness and how it can be treated.

Depression is a disease of the brain that affects the entire mind and body. It makes the person feel miserable. It can also make them feel tired, no matter how much rest they have had. Does it make a person crazy? No, but it might make them think they are.

What causes depression? We can't be sure, it seems to have lots of causes. It might be because a person doesn't have the skills to cope with severe psychological stress. But normal, healthy people can also become depressed so sometimes the cause could be chemical or hereditary.

Mental illness, like physical illness, affects people differently. However, because there is no outward sign of injury, the ordinary person might misunderstand their behaviour. A friend can help by accepting the 'strange' behaviour that is part of the illness and showing other people that it isn't dangerous or threatening.

Often people who are thinking of killing themselves need to talk things through with someone who will not judge them, but they may

Depression is very common, about 1 in 4 people may become clinically depressed at some point

not be sure how to start or who they can trust. Let them know you will listen, you won't tell them they are stupid, and you won't talk to other people about them. However, it's just as important to let them know that you can't keep a secret if it means they might seriously harm themselves, a teacher or a relative might need to be told if they say they are going to kill themselves.

If someone cuts themselves, they might not be suicidal. Many young people use this behaviour as a way of feeling in control. They are still in need of good friends and might want someone to talk to, someone who isn't going to say they're going mad.

It's OK to ask the person, 'Do you ever feel so badly that you think of suicide?' Don't worry about planting the idea in someone's head. Suicidal thoughts are common with depressive illnesses, although not all people have them. If a person has been thinking of suicide, they will be relieved and grateful that you were willing to be so open and non-judgmental. It shows a person you truly care and take them seriously.

■ The above information is from Papyrus' web site which can be found at www.papyrus-uk.org

Fight for survival

Could student suicides be prevented with better targeting of support services?

By Kate Coxon

The effects of a student suicide reverberate far beyond the individual death. According to Nicky Stanley, senior lecturer in social work at the University of Hull: 'Parents, relatives, close friends, students on the same programme, academic staff, student support staff, accommodation staff and student union officers will all wonder what they could have done to prevent the death and experience strong feelings of loss.'

Two cases this summer caused a flurry of attention – a recent inquest into the death of a Cardiff University student recorded a verdict of suicide, and the parents of a Cambridge student blamed malaria medication for their daughter's apparent suicide. But are students more at risk than others?

No, says Dr Mike Hobbs, consultant psychiatrist at the Warneford Hospital, Oxford. 'Studies in Oxford, Cambridge and Edinburgh have tracked student suicides over a number of years and the research to date does not suggest high numbers at all.' He adds: 'Although suicides at certain institutions have always interested the media, rates of suicide among students are no higher than among the general population. In fact, evidence suggests the suicide rate in students is lower than that in the age-matched population, but this does not mean we can afford to be complacent.'

Dr Hobbs points out, however, that reports in recent years suggest that university counsellors are seeing more students with mental health problems. 'There is also a perception that, in some students, these problems are more severe than was seen previously.'

> **Involving young people themselves in suicide prevention strategies is thought to reduce the stigma of seeking help**

Concerns about student mental health including suicide and self-harm prompted a coalition of 10 voluntary organisations, including the Samaritans, Mind and the National Union of Students, to approach the Committee of Vice-Chancellors and Principals (now Universities UK) in March 1999 to undertake research into student suicide. Its aim was to establish trends and collate examples of good practice in suicide prevention.

It hasn't gone according to plan. Policy guidelines are to be published, but not figures. Kerry Napuk, coordinator of the University Suicide Initiative and a member of Papyrus (Parents' Association for the Prevention of Young Suicide) is concerned that policy guidelines may not go far enough. 'I believe the focus of this research has been altered, delayed and diminished, but I'm hopeful that we can have a positive outcome if universities are able to communicate and share their experiences to develop universal good practice.'

Diana Warwick, chief executive of Universities UK, said universities offered a wide range of support. 'Universities UK is committed to the dissemination of good practice across the sector, and is currently producing a set of policy guidelines drawn from our research into student suicide, to be published in early 2003.'

The Samaritans estimate that around 6,000 people take their own lives each year – a rate of around 11 per 100,000 people. But a major difficulty is the lack of valid and conclusive data on the extent of the problem of student suicide. The Office of National Statistics, which collects data on suicide rates, does not supply information on student suicides, nor is this information collected by the Higher Education Statistical Agency. In a climate where universities are competing for students, and for funding, institutions are unlikely to voluntarily publish figures on student suicides. Some believe that simply logging the numbers of student suicides may not be helpful.

But there are other complications. Students tend to have more than one residence. 'If a student dies in a vacation, is it appropriate

for an institution to pursue a distressed family to find out the precise cause of death?' asks Annie Grant, director of the educational development and support centre at the University of Leicester.

But Anna Brown, director-trustee of Papyrus, insists: 'We need to know more about these students, whether they are full-time or part-time, and we also need a breakdown of the figures between further and higher education. We need to know which groups of students are most at risk and how they can best be targeted for support services.'

As a new academic year begins, student mental health appears to be high on the agenda. A working party set up by the Royal College of Psychiatrists will soon publish a report into student mental health. Universities UK is currently undertaking a student services project, with publication due later this autumn. But reports and recommendations need to be matched by funding, argues Verity Coyle, welfare officer for the National Union of Students. She points out that there is still tremendous variety in student support provision and in waiting times across institutions. 'It's of great concern to us that some students might pluck up the courage to get to a counsellor only to find they have to wait 12 to 14 weeks to actually see one,' she says. Many student support services have expanded, but others are under pressure. Last year South Bank University cut its counselling service.

Involving young people themselves in suicide prevention strategies is thought to reduce the stigma of seeking help. Papyrus has just produced a new leaflet, *Thinking of ending it all*, for young people, by young people. Initiatives which involve other students – such as mentoring schemes and awareness-raising campaigns – are gaining momentum across the sector.

With funding from a Mind Millennium award, Natasha Don-nelly has just set up the Studentsinmind project, which will design and create a national website and a confidential email signposting service for students in higher education. 'Students, especially male students, may be more inclined to make an initial contact via email than by a face-to-face consultation,' she says. Student volunteers who have experienced mental distress and been fully trained by the London Samaritans will respond to the emails.

■ The Samaritans: 08457 909090 or email jo@samaritans.org Nightline: visit www.nightline.org.uk www.niss.ac.uk for details of local services. Papyrus: leaflets available from Papyrus, Rossendale GH, Union Road, Rawtenstall, Lancs BB4 6NE. Tel/Fax: 01706 214449, email: infor@papyrus-uk.org www.studentsinmind.org.uk

■ This article first appeared in *The Guardian*, September 2002.
© Kate Coxon

Suicide

Information from CALM

If you're feeling hopeless about the future, or believe that no one cares about you, you are not alone. Suicide is now the biggest killer of young men in England and Wales. The very fact that so many young men take their life shows it's much more common than society likes to admit. But this doesn't mean it's the answer for you.

A huge step like suicide is not to be taken lightly or hastily. Don't burden yourself by trying to deal with things on your own. Just talking it through could be the release you're looking for.

Tell someone you trust, let them know how you're feeling. Or you could call CALM. We won't judge or argue with you. And we can put you in touch with groups that can help you further.

Suicidal thoughts can come into your head:
■ For no reason at all. This is very frightening and sometimes happens because some of the chemicals in your brain are not working properly.
■ Because something has happened which has upset you a great deal.
■ When someone close to you has attempted or actually committed suicide.
■ Because you have been using drugs or drinking heavily.

■ Or because of a combination of any of these things.

Suicidal thoughts can happen to anybody. It's hard to generalise but many people who think about taking their own lives:
■ are very sensitive to failure or criticism
■ set themselves targets which are difficult to achieve
■ find it hard to cope with disappointment
■ find it difficult to admit to having problems they don't know how to solve
■ find it hard to tell others how they are feeling

Most suicidal people don't actually want to die, but are looking for an answer to their problems, an end to their pain and despair. Suicide can seem the only way out. It is a decision made when other decisions seem impossible.

If you feel worthless, hopeless about the future, or believe that no one cares about you – or even that the world would be a better place without you – talk to CALM. We're here to listen, not to judge, and could offer you the support you need to stop feeling this way.
■ The above information is from CALM's web site, based on *Thinking of Ending it All?* published by Papyrus. Visit CALM's web site at www.thecalmzone.net Or call them on 0800 58 58 58.
© CALM

Deliberate self-harm in young people

Deliberate self-harm is a term used when someone intentionally injures or harms themselves. Common examples include 'overdosing' (self-poisoning), hitting, cutting or burning oneself, pulling hair or picking skin, and self-strangulation. It can also include taking illegal drugs and excessive amounts of alcohol. Self-harm is always a sign of something being seriously wrong.

How often does it happen?

It's hard to say exactly, because most people keep their self-harm very private. Some say as many as 1 teenager in 10 could be affected. Health professionals probably see only the tip of the iceberg, and certainly nothing like this number. The problem mainly affects girls and is rare in boys (7:1 female:male ratio). It is very much more common than suicide.

Why do young people harm themselves?

It is not necessarily attention-seeking. Self-injury is a way of dealing with very difficult feelings that build up inside. People say different things about why they do it. Some say that they have been feeling desperate about a problem and don't know where to turn for help. They feel trapped and helpless. Self-injury helps them to feel more in control. Others talk of feelings of anger or tension that get bottled up inside until they feel like exploding. Self-injuring relieves this tension. Feelings of guilt or shame may also become unbearable. Self-harm is a way of punishing oneself. Some people try to cope with very upsetting experiences like trauma or abuse by convincing themselves that the upsetting event(s) never happened. These people sometimes suffer from feelings of numbness or deadness. They say that they feel detached from the world and their bodies, and that self-injury is a way of feeling more connected and alive.

Self-injury is always a sign of great upset. Sometimes people can end up killing themselves accidentally. The difficult feelings that lead to self-harm can be caused by a number of things. Young people who are depressed or have an eating disorder are at risk. So are people who take illegal drugs or excessive amounts of alcohol. In fact, eating

---

> *Self-injury is always a sign of great upset. Sometimes people can end up killing themselves accidentally*

---

disorders and drug or alcohol misuse are a kind of self-harm in themselves. The commonest trigger is an argument with a parent or close friend. When family life involves a lot of abuse, neglect or rejection, people are more likely to harm themselves. 'Copy cat' self-harm sometimes happens in a group. It can have tragic results.

Why they need help

Anyone who is harming themselves is struggling to cope and needs help. If people don't get help when they need it, problems are likely to continue. Problems may also get a lot worse and the effects may 'snowball'. Some people will continue to harm themselves more and more seriously. They may even end up killing themselves.

What can you do to help?

A person who is thinking of killing themselves often tries to let someone else know how upset they are. They are most likely to share their upset feelings with friends of their own age or adults they know well. But self-injury is different and is often kept

secret – even from friends or family. The person feels so ashamed, guilty or bad that they can't face talking about it. There may be clues, such as refusing to wear short sleeves or take off jumpers for games.

If you are a parent or teacher, you can help by:

- recognising signs of distress and finding some way of talking with the young person about how they are feeling.
- listening to their worries and problems and taking them seriously.
- offering sympathy and understanding.
- helping with solving problems.
- staying calm and constructive – however upset you feel about the self-harm.
- being clear about the risks of self-harm – making sure they know that, with help, it will be possible to stop once the underlying problems have been sorted out.
- making sure that they get the right kind of help as soon as possible.

It's important to make sure that the young person feels that they have someone they can talk to and get support from when they need it. If they can't get it when they need it, there is a risk they will harm themselves instead. It's important to ask whether parents and family will be able to give the support that's needed. This may be difficult if there are a lot of problems or arguments at home. As a parent, you may be too upset or angry to be able to give the help that is needed. If so, you should seek advice from your family doctor.

If you are a teacher, it is important to encourage students to let you know if one of their group is in trouble, upset or shows signs of harming themselves. Because friends often worry about betraying a confidence, you may need to explain that self-harm can be dangerous to life. For this reason it should never be kept secret. It's better to get help than to suffer in silence.

Specialist help available

If you feel that more professional help is needed, the family doctor should be able to advise. They will

---

Type and reasons for deliberate self-harm

	Men	Women	All
How harmed self*			
Cut self	59%	66%	63%
Swallowed object	12%	15%	14%
Burnt self	4%	8%	6%
Harmed self in other way	38%	28%	32%
Reason for self-harm*			
To draw attention	58%	54%	56%
Because of anger	68%	80%	75%
Base	71	122	193

* Respondents could give more than one answer   Source: Crown copyright

---

be able to tell you what help is available locally and make a referral to your local child and adolescent mental health service. Here the team includes child psychiatrists, psychologists, social workers, psychotherapists and specialist nurses who can offer expert help.

Many young people who harm themselves do need specialist help. *Everyone* who has taken an overdose needs an urgent assessment by a doctor as soon as possible, even if they look OK. The harmful effects can sometimes be delayed. Even small amounts of some medications can be fatal.

All young people who need hospital treatment for self-harm should have a specialist mental health assessment. Often, this will be done by a child and adolescent psychiatrist in a community clinic or

---

It's important to make sure that the young person feels that they have someone they can talk to and get support from when they need it

---

hospital. The aim is to discover the causes of the problems and to prevent repetition. It is very helpful when parents or carers can take part. This makes it easier to understand the background to what has happened, and to work out what sort of help is needed after the young person leaves hospital.

Psychological treatment can make all the difference. There are different approaches, depending on what is causing the problem. It often involves both individual and family work. Individuals will need help with how to cope with the very difficult feelings that cause self-harm. Families often need help in working out how to make sure that the dangerous behaviour doesn't happen again, and how to give the support that is needed. If depression or anxiety are part of the problem, medication may be helpful. Occasionally, intensive help may be needed. Sometimes recovery from very damaging or traumatic experiences happens slowly. Then specialist help is needed over a longer period of time.

- The above information is from the Royal College of Psychiatrists' web site which can be found at www.rcpsych.ac.uk

Treating the stigma

Initiative to change A&E staff attitudes to self-harmers

By David Batty

Imagine turning up at hospital in severe pain, only to be roughly handled by doctors and nurses who say you are wasting their time. This was what faced Mark Smith during the 13 years that he deliberately injured himself. As a result, he felt more worthless and less likely to seek help – with near tragic consequences.

'My treatment from staff in Accident & Emergency departments varied fro2m indifferent to downright vicious and humiliating,' he recalls. 'This ranged from doctors telling me I was wasting bed space, to having strips put on wounds – instead of stitches – and being kept waiting for hours.'

Smith, 31, is now a community mental health worker in Nottingham for the National Schizophrenia Fellowship (NSF), the mental health charity. He works at Churchill House, which provides residential care and telephone support for people in mental distress.

'My worst experience was in casualty in Derby in November, 1995,' he says. 'The doctor put a drip in my hand extremely roughly, even though I didn't want one. She then wheeled me into a side room on a trolley and left me in a room with a box full of razor blades.'

Deliberate self-harm leads to about 150,000 attendances at A&E every year and is one of the top five causes of acute medical admission. But research for the health standards watchdog, the national institute for clinical excellence (Nice), reveals that more than half all self-harmers are discharged without a psychiatric assessment and face negative attitudes from healthcare staff.

Smith hopes to combat this stigma by running self-harm workshops for A&E and mental health staff to dispel myths about the condition. The training sessions, which will be piloted within the NSF from next month, will explore why people self-harm and will challenge the idea that it is mere attention-seeking. Smith deliberately injured himself after years of bullying and racist abuse.

'Self-harm is a cry for help, in the sense that you can't express your distress in any other way, but it's not attention seeking,' he says. 'Most self-harmers are ashamed of, and frightened by, what they do. They hide their scars, cutting parts of the body no one can see, wearing long sleeves, or using make-up on their arms. There's often a deep feeling of calm and relief immediately after cutting, although that's rapidly replaced by an overwhelming sense of guilt and revulsion.'

Deliberate self-harm leads to about 150,000 attendances at A&E every year

The workshops – based on role-playing exercises, with staff taking the part of patients – emphasise the value of non-judgmental support. 'Most self-harmers dread going to casualty for fear of how staff will react,' Smith says. 'The first time I went to hospital, I was terrified. I got a lecture from a nurse, who made it clear I should be ashamed, which only reinforced my feelings of self-loathing.'

He also wants staff to think about their attitudes towards other, more socially acceptable self-

harming behaviours, such as smoking and taking drugs. 'They wouldn't treat someone with lung cancer or cirrhosis of the liver in the same way,' he says. 'And doctors and nurses suffer high levels of substance abuse.'

The NSF initiative is welcomed by experts working to improve the treatment of self-harm. Mike Smith, former director of nursing at North Birmingham mental health trust, who runs courses on managing the condition, says that 'almost all doctors and nurses feel terrible when they reflect on how they've treated self-harmers'.

He adds: 'Often, A&E staff react negatively because they're stressed out dealing with many serious injuries, from a granny who's been beaten up to a child burned in a house fire, so someone who's cut themselves may not be regarded as deserving the same priority. They also feel useless as the same people keep turning up. I advise them to simply regard admission as an opportunity to let people know that someone cares.'

Mark Smith hopes that national guidelines on the management and prevention of self-harm, currently under development by Nice, will ensure patients are in future treated with dignity, privacy and respect.

Consultant psychiatrist Tim Kendall, co-director of the Royal College of Psychiatrists' national collaborating centre for mental health, which aims to complete the guidance by 2004, says: 'People who harm themselves are often treated as less than human. A minority of staff are aggressive, telling patients they've brought their distress on themselves, which is very traumatic.

'The guidance will tackle that stigma and promote positive practice. There is evidence that, if you can help someone 48 hours after they've self-harmed, then you can reduce the long-term risk of harm and suicide.'

Worried about self-injury?

Information from YoungMinds

What is self-injury?

Self-injury is a way of dealing with very difficult feelings that build up inside. People deal with these feelings in various ways. Here are some examples:

- Cutting or burning themselves
- Bruising themselves
- Taking an overdose of tablets
- Pulling hair, or picking skin.

Some people think that the seriousness of the problem can be measured by how bad the injury is. This is not the case – a person who hurts themselves a bit can be feeling just as bad as someone who hurts themselves a lot.

Self-injury can affect anyone. It is a lot more common than people think. Many people hurt themselves secretly for a long time before finding the courage to tell someone.

Why do people do it?

'I think control's a big thing. You can't control what's happening around you, but you can control what you do to yourself.'

Everyone has problems in their lives and often people look for help. But sometimes it's hard to cope or even to put feelings into words. If they get bottled up inside, the pressure goes up and up until they feel like they might explode. This is the point where some people injure themselves.

'I didn't think there was any way out of my situation, so I took loads of tablets. I felt so bad I just wanted to die . . . and I nearly did. Now things are different, and I'm so glad to be alive.'

What makes people so stressed?

There are lots of things:

- Bullying
- Bereavement
- Housing problems
- Abuse
- Problems to do with race, culture or religion
- Growing up
- Money
- Pressure to fit in
- Sexual feelings
- Problems with friends
- Pressures at school or work

When a lot of problems come together, they can feel too much. If you're also feeling vulnerable, it's hard to cope as well as you normally do.

Thinking about stopping

There are lots of reasons why you might want to stop injuring yourself, although you might not know what else to do to help you cope. Here are some feelings that you might recognise . . .

- Hating yourself . . . for not being what people want
- Afraid . . . that you might end up dead
- Guilty . . . because you can't stop harming yourself, even if you want to
- Helpless . . . you don't know what to do for the best
- Embarrassed . . . in case people think you're weird
- Isolated . . . you don't know who to talk to
- Depressed . . . about anything ever getting better
- Out of control . . . you might not know why you hurt yourself and wonder if you're going mad
- Upset . . . you can't keep your feelings in . . . or maybe you can't let them out
- Scared . . . because you don't know why you do it . . . it's getting worse
- Worried . . . in case people think you're 'just attention-seeking'

'It helps a lot when I can be with someone I trust. I need people to understand me, support me. I need to be treated normally – just like anyone else. Not like a mad person. I'm not mad. I've just got problems because of what happened in my past. Something happens – and suddenly all the memories and feelings come back.'

When self-injury becomes a way of coping with stress it is a sign that there are problems that need sorting out. Help or support may be needed from family, friends, or others.

Helping yourself

If you have worries that make you want to injure yourself, you might want help to change. This section is about what you can do to help yourself.

Thinking about why you do it

Lots of people don't know why they harm themselves and it can be scary to become aware of how you feel and why. Stopping self-injury is easier if you can find other ways of coping. To do this, you'll first need to have a clear idea of why you do it. Many people find it useful to talk to someone who is trained to help.

Here are some questions that may be helpful for you to think about:

- What was happening when you first began to feel like injuring yourself?
- What seems to trigger the feeling of wanting to hurt yourself now?
- Are you always at a certain place or with a particular person?
- Do you have frightening memories or thoughts and feel you can't tell anyone?
- Is there anything else that makes you want to hurt yourself?

What helps you not hurt yourself?

When you feel upset, what helps you to cope? Some people find it helpful to be with a friend, talk to someone they trust, make a phone call, exercise, or do something else they enjoy. Others find it helps to paint or draw, listen to music or write feelings down in a diary or letter (even if it's not to send). *What helps you?*

Deciding to get help

Sometimes, however hard you try to stop injuring yourself on your own, you can't.

'The feeling of wanting to hurt myself would build up. I could put off doing it for a while but I couldn't last for ever. I knew I had to get help.'

If you feel like this, it probably means that you need to talk to someone you can trust. This needs to be someone who will listen to you, talk about how you feel and give practical help. There could be a real risk that you could harm yourself permanently or perhaps even die.

If you feel your life is in danger it is very important to get help. You can make an emergency appointment to see your doctor.

Who can you trust to listen?

'Cutting myself is such a private thing.

I find it hard to talk to other people about how I feel. They don't understand. They think I'm seeking attention – that's the last thing I want.'

When you have thought of someone to talk to, it helps to be prepared:
1. Where and when would you tell them?
2. Would you tell them face to face, by phone, or letter?
3. What would you say?
4. You could practise by saying it out loud, somewhere you feel safe
5. Picture how the person might respond if you told them

Think of a way to look after yourself if they respond in a way which isn't what you'd hoped. Remember, the first person you speak to might not be able to help. This may not be their fault – or yours. Don't give up – it does matter that you try again.

What if you can't talk to someone you know?

If there is no one you feel you can trust at the moment, you could try a telephone helpline. They can be very helpful when there's no one else you can turn to. They can make you feel more relaxed and able to speak than you might think – and it's up to you when you finish the conversation.

It's sometimes easier to talk to someone trained to help, who doesn't know you.

There are a lot of places that offer advice and help. You could contact a youth counselling service.

Your doctor or school nurse should be able to advise you about what support is available locally. They could refer you to someone who has experience of helping people who self-injure.

'What helped was having someone to talk to who was reliable and didn't rush me. I haven't done anything to myself for ages now. Sometimes I feel like it, but I don't need to do it any more, and the feeling goes.'

The person you see will want to help – and won't think you are stupid, mad or wasting their time. The service is confidential (they should explain what this means and also the rare times when they will have to tell someone else) – no one else will know what you've

talked about. They are used to talking to people who have all sorts of worries. They can help you work out what's bothering you, even if you're not sure what to say. Although it can take a lot of courage and determination, it's important to keep trying. You will find the right person to help you in the end.

Friends and family – how you can help

'Cutting was always a very secret thing . . . You feel so ashamed, so bad about yourself. You feel no one will ever understand.'

If you are worried about someone who is self-injuring and want to help, this section tells you some things you can do.

Friends and family have a really important part to play. You can help by:
- Noticing that someone is self-injuring
- Offering to listen and support
- Getting help when it's needed

It may be difficult to understand why someone injures themselves. You may feel shocked, angry or even guilty. It can also be hard to know how to help.

Here are some suggestions:

- Keep an open mind – don't judge or jump to conclusions
- Make time to listen and take them seriously
- Help them to find their own way of managing their problems
- Help them work out who else can help
- Offer to go with them to tell someone, or offer to tell someone for them
- Carry on with the ordinary activities you do together
- Don't be offended if they don't want to handle things your way
- Don't tease them – respect their feelings
- Support any positive steps they take

What to do if the situation looks dangerous

'She made me swear I wouldn't tell anyone. I knew if I did she would have hated my guts. On the other hand, if I didn't, she could have died and I would

have felt it was my fault. I did tell someone, but she wouldn't speak to me after.'

Someone may tell you that they are hurting themselves and ask you to keep it a secret. This can put you in a very difficult situation. Of course, it's important to respect their wish for privacy. But if you think their life is in danger it is important to get help as soon as you can.

You may be able to work out together who would be the best person to tell. If not, try and let them know that you had to tell someone, and why.

It's important to remember that your feelings matter too . . .

- Look after yourself – make sure you get the support you need

- Remember – even those trained to work with people who self-injure need support, so it's OK if you do too
- Try to carry on with your other activities and relationships
- You don't have to be available for them all the time
- If they hurt themselves it is not because of you, even if they say it is

■ The above information is from *Worried about self-injury?* published by YoungMinds. This colourful, pocket-sized booklet aims to help young people understand more about what self-injury is, why people do it, and to help people find support for them-selves or people they know. By using genuine quotes from young people who have self-injured, the booklet gets to grips with what self-injury means to those who do it, and what approaches can help people to think about stopping. The booklet also lists the addresses and telephone numbers of organisations which young people can contact if they need further help. Price: 55p each.

YoungMinds would like to thank 42nd Street for permission to use quotes from their book *Who's hurting who?* The book is available from 42nd Street, 2nd Floor, Swan Building, 20 Swan Street, Manchester, M4 5JW. 0161 832 0170.
■ The above information is from YoungMind's web site which can be found at www.youngminds.org.uk

© YoungMinds

One in ten teenagers self-harm

Schools might have to screen pupils for their potential to self-harm after a survey of 6,000 teenagers revealed one in 10 had tried to hurt themselves, mostly through cutting or poisoning.

Research for the Samaritans charity also revealed that girls were four times more likely than boys to have tried self-harm, a tendency that was more marked in white or mixed-race young people than those from black or Asian backgrounds.

Anonymous questionnaires completed by 15- and 16-year-olds in 41 schools in Birmingham, Oxfordshire and Northamptonshire suggested that they were reluctant to turn to teachers, voluntary organisa-tions and relatives, preferring to rely on friends for support.

The study, by the centre for suicide research at Oxford University, also found that the risk of teenagers trying to poison or injure themselves significantly increased if they had friends who had done the same.

Samaritans commissioned the work partly because it is known that adolescents who self-harm are far more likely to go on to die by suicide.

By James Meikle, Health Correspondent

Young people who had attempted self-harm were more likely to say they did it to get relief from a 'terrible state of mind' or they wanted to die than to get their own back, frighten someone or get attention. Many had also suffered problems with schoolwork or family illness.

Girls were found to be four times more likely than boys to have tried self-harm

More than 24,000 teenagers are taken to hospital in Britain each year after deliberately harming them-selves, mostly through drug overdoses or cutting themselves. But only one in eight incidents described by teenagers in the survey led to hospital treatment – suggesting the problem is far more widespread.

This discrepancy may be explained by the preference of those self-harming to cut themselves, as minor cuts are less likely to require hospital treatment.

The survey found 10.3% of pupils reported they had harmed themselves at some time, 6.9% had done so in the previous year and 2.5% in the previous month.

The report, published at a conference in London in March 2003, said: 'Since the vast majority of pupils who self-harm do not go to hospital, prevention needs to take place in the community, ideally within the school.'

Pupils might need better educational programmes to promote psychological well-being, while teachers needed to recognise pupils getting into difficulties, it added. 'A more controversial approach that might be considered is the use of screening in schools to detect those pupils at risk.'

■ Samaritans can be contacted on their telephone helpline: 08457 909090 or by email: jo@samaritans.org
© Guardian Newspapers Limited 2003

Young men speak

Information from the Samaritans

The concern

Suicide among young people is a phenomenon both puzzling and worrying. The rates of male suicide in all age groups and in most countries have shown a striking increase since the 1970s but this is most marked in the 15 to 24 year age group. In many parts of the world it had become the second most frequent cause of death after accident, among the 15 to 24 year age group.

What we need to know

. . . despite the considerable volume of research and clinical work on adolescent suicidal behaviour, there is still a long way to go in explaining the upward secular trend and in finding effective methods of pre-vention . . . possible explanations that are worthy of further study . . . are . . . the role of depression in suicide; the increase in use of alcohol and psycho-active drugs; the possible role of antisocial behaviour; the possible increase in family conflict; the decline in parental support associated with changes in family structures; the possible effect of an extended period of social dependency during adolescence; and the likely role of changing circumstances in society as a whole.

This study views adolescent depression and suicidal behaviour from the perspective of young men themselves. From a national survey of more than 1,300 young men, two groups were identified: a wider depressed group (of 152 people) who admitted to feeling depressed often or to having suicidal thoughts or to having attempted suicide; and a smaller suicidal group (40 people) who admitted to feeling depressed often and thought about killing themselves, and had actually attempted it. The findings show how these young men's perceptions of themselves, their families and their schools differed from those who did not have such feelings. The study adds another piece to the jigsaw of research on adolescent suicide and depression. This information will be

useful to the Samaritans and other agencies in their continuing work preventing unnecessary deaths in young people.

The survey covered a range of issues in the lives of boys and young men. Four domains were explored, the self, the family, school and community and the wider world. The findings show that young men who felt depressed or suicidal had very different perceptions about themselves and different experiences in their families and at school from those who did not feel this way. An increased risk of depression or suicidal feelings was noted with each successive year of adolescence. Some of the key findings are highlighted here.

'Boys don't talk about problems or phone helplines as much after eleven (years old) 'cos we're supposed to be becoming more manly, many feel it's time to stop relying on other people. Deal with it themselves. There is influence from older boys, and teachers maybe treat them like they're a child and say "Don't be so silly" and you get reluctant to ask, you might be laughed at. I would confide in my friends, I could trust my friends and I could listen and be sympathetic. I'd try and sort them out. I would tell a girl emotional and family things.' 14 Surrey

Summary of findings

Violence and bullying

Some of the most significant differences between the depressed and non-depressed and suicidal and non-suicidal lay in their experience and use of violence. With extensive experience of violence in their lives at home and at school, and the addition of bullying outside of school, it was not surprising that they were more likely to react with anti-social or violent actions when distressed themselves. More than a third of the suicidal group would smash something if they were very worried or upset. Many pick fights. 60% of the suicidal group said 'bullying is affecting my life' and 69% said they had 'experienced violence from an adult'. Half of the suicidal group reported having been in trouble with the police compared to 17% of the non-suicidal.

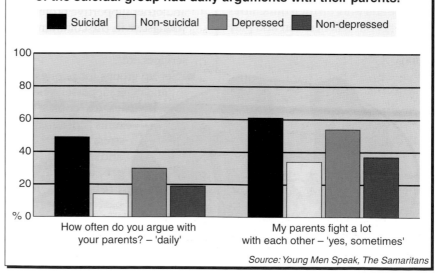

Family conflict

More suicidal than non-suicidal and depressed than non-depressed young men felt that their parents fought a lot with each other. Half of the suicidal group had daily arguments with their parents.

Legend: ■ Suicidal □ Non-suicidal ▨ Depressed ▦ Non-depressed

How often do you argue with your parents? – 'daily'

My parents fight a lot with each other – 'yes, sometimes'

Source: Young Men Speak, The Samaritans

Anti-social behaviour

This was a frequent consequence of being worried or upset. Suicidal young men were four times more likely to smash something up than non-suicidal. The suicidal group were also significantly more likely to 'keep it to myself' and 'stay in my room'. The depressed and suicidal groups were significantly more likely to have been in trouble with the police than their non-depressed counterparts.

Drugs, alcohol and cigarettes

Depressed and suicidal boys resort to drugs, alcohol and cigarettes to a much greater extent than their counterparts who do not feel depressed. Suicidal young men were ten times more likely to use a drug to relieve stress. They also report receiving less clear and useful information on drugs from parents and schools. Access to better information and reassurance might alleviate some of these anxieties.

Living arrangements

Significant differences were found in residence patterns between non-depressed and depressed young people who were less likely to be living with two parents. Suicidal young people were eight times more likely than non-suicidal counterparts to be living alone, in care or hostels or without a family structure.

Family lives

Family lives reflected a negative parenting style, few sources of emotional support, little family togetherness, such as to eat a meal or go to visit relatives together.

Fathers

Suicidal respondents were significantly more likely to have 'a father who is absent but I see him'. Among the suicidal group, 41% said their fathers lived elsewhere but saw their sons, compared to 18% of the non-suicidal boys. Stepfathers were common to both depressed and suicidal groups. Merely living with a father was not in itself enough. The father/son relationship was found to be significant for both suicidal and depressed young men in the extent to which a father talked through worries with his son and talked about relationships with him. The suicidal group were significantly more likely to believe their father 'wanted them to fight their own battles'.

Mothers

Mothers were an important source of emotional support for boys who did not often choose to confide in friends. Therefore when this support was not available, the lack of it was highlighted.

Parents' relationships

Large numbers of boys in all groups felt anxious about their parents' relationships but these worries were more pronounced in the depressed and suicidal groups.

Sources of support

67% of people in the suicidal group replied that they turned 'nowhere' for emotional support. A third or more of the depressed and suicidal were likely to use ChildLine or the Samaritans as a source of emotional support.

The future

These young men are less certain that Britain is a good place to grow up in. Future aspirations are not thought likely to be achieved by depressed and suicidal groups. 'There are no jobs' is given as a powerful reason. However, it is noted that around a quarter of the depressed and suicidal groups say 'I have been talked out of it' in contrast to only 5% of the non-suicidal group.

Gender issues

To young men with low self esteem, gender equality issues present difficulties. The depressed and suicidal group were less likely to agree that 'Women's equality is a good thing', and almost two-thirds of suicidal boys believe 'it was easier when roles were clearly separate'. There are high levels of family conflict in the lives of a large number of depressed and suicidal boys and it is possible that their views of gender equality emanate in part from what they see within the family, increased by their own sense of worthlessness. Gender-specific factors are found among barriers young men describe when it comes to getting help. They report powerful myths about what a man does or does not do which restrict their options. A dual life was described in which a front or shell hid an inner turmoil until 'barriers collapse and it all falls apart'. Expectations from the society around them, both their peers and older males, acted as an added pressure. The widely held view was that seeking help placed you in a vulnerable or weak position. Suicidal boys were more likely to have a father who 'insists you fight your own battles'.

School

Significantly fewer of the depressed group liked school, or felt that school was 'OK most of the time'. Fewer liked their teachers. They were also significantly less likely to take their work seriously, and more likely to feel their teacher 'made them feel stupid when they made a mistake'. The suicidal group reflected many of these findings regarding school.

The way forward

Creative suggestions include ways of making a service more attractive to young men, and ideas which reduce the 'talk based' component for those who find talking so difficult. Reducing the stigma widely felt by young men towards asking for help was thought to be vital, and providing greater understanding of how professional and voluntary services such as helplines actually work was recommended for young people in general.

Crime prevention strategies frequently consider family support, school-based support and leisure and recreation schemes with various criminal justice interventions. They do not always include attention to mental health. However, the high percentage of suicidal young men who report having been in trouble with the police suggests that linked work on mental health services for this age group may be more useful than punishment.

■ The above information is from the publication *Young Men Speak* by the Samaritans. For more information visit their web site at www.samaritans.org.uk

© Samaritans

Thinking of ending it all?

If you have been thinking about taking your own life or have already tried to do it, this information should help you on the road to feeling better

Why do you feel like this ?

Lots of young people feel suicidal at some point in their lives. Thousands go into hospital each year having tried to harm themselves. Many more than this try to take their own lives – and nobody ever gets to know about it.

Most of them recover and never try again. A small number, however, do succeed in killing themselves.

This is why feeling suicidal can be dangerous and needs to be talked about.

Suicidal thoughts can come into your head . . . for no reason at all

This is very frightening and some-times happens because some of the chemicals in your brain are not working properly. You may have an illness called depression which you will need to talk to your doctor about . . . because something has happened to you which has upset you a great deal. Like for example:

- splitting up with a boyfriend or girlfriend
- being bullied
- feeling ashamed of something you've done
- feeling ashamed of something that was not your fault
- someone close to you has died
- not getting the exam results you wanted
- feeling confused about your sexuality
- feeling you can't live up to other people's expectations
- problems at home
- because you have been using drugs or drinking heavily.
- when someone close to you has attempted or actually committed suicide.
- or because of a combination of any of these things

What kind of person feels like this ?

It can happen to anybody.

It's very hard to generalise about this, but many young people who think about taking their own lives

- are very sensitive to failure or criticism
- set themselves targets which are difficult to achieve
- cannot cope well with dis-appointment
- find it difficult to admit to having problems and don't know how to solve them
- find it hard to tell others how they are feeling

They often feel worthless, feel hopeless about the future, or believe that no one cares about them, even that the world would be a better place without them.

Friends and family may be seeing someone who on the outside . . .

- is very angry and hostile
- has become very quiet and withdrawn
- is the life and soul of the party
- seems no different from usual,
      . . . but they have no idea how you are feeling inside.

Many young people don't actually want to die, but are looking for an answer to their problems, an end to their pain and despair – and suicide can seem to be the only way out.

When this state of mind has been reached, it is impossible to think straight (although you will believe that you're thinking clearly) and things can get totally out of proportion.

How do you know if you've got depression ?

Just like physical illness, mental health problems can vary from mild to serious. Most people who suffer a bout of psychological illness will go on to make a complete recovery.

Anxiety and depression are very common and both can be successfully treated.

Depression, however, can kill – if suicidal thoughts get the better of you. You may be feeling:

- tired all the time
- sad and miserable
- can't be bothered to do things
- inadequate
- tearful
- anxious
- panicky
- agitated
- scared people will laugh at you
- that you're going mad
- like shit!

Perhaps you've:

- lost interest in food
- found it difficult to concentrate

Social functioning characteristics

Of those who had never deliberately harmed themselves, 17% had experienced six or more stressful events, 8% had a severe lack of social support.

	Lifetime deliberate self-harm		
	Yes	No	All
Relationship problems, illness and bereavement	%	%	%
Death of close friend/other relative	70	64	64
Death of close relative	37	53	53
Serious illness, injury or assault	47	23	26
Serious illness, injury or assault to close relative	33	23	24
Separation or divorce	36	22	22
Serious problem with close friend/relative	21	12	12
None of these	2	9	9
Base	197	8321	8518

Source: Crown copyright

- lost your confidence
- lost interest in other things too – hobbies, sport, your appearance
- stopped going out with friends

You must go to see your doctor who will be able to tell you if you are depressed, and will know what to do to help you to get back to normal.

What happens if you go ahead?

Sometimes the person who attempts suicide does not die but damages their body so badly that full recovery is impossible.

If you take your own life, there is no turning back, no second chance. Death is final.

It can be extremely traumatic for the person who finds your body. Something they will never forget.

The effect of suicide on family and friends can be overwhelming. Of all the different ways of dying, suicide is the most difficult for those who are left behind to cope with – whether they are parents, children, partners, friends or even acquaintances.

You won't be around to help other people who may be feeling just as bad as you have done.

You have prevented other people from helping you – for ever.

So what can you do about it ?

Tell someone you trust how you are feeling. This could be someone in your family, your doctor, a teacher, the school nurse, college counsellor . . . If the person you are telling doesn't seem to understand, don't be put off – tell someone else. You could phone a helpline. If you reach a suicidal crisis where the desire to kill yourself is overwhelming, you must tell someone. Ask them to keep you company until the feelings pass.

Thinking bad thoughts about yourself all the time (especially about killing yourself) makes you feel worse. You might be thinking that you're a failure or nobody likes you or that nothing will get better. There might be some thoughts that are very private to you.

Try to recognise when your bad thoughts are likely to come and prepare for them. Try to find something that will get rid of them or will make you think about them

Don't expect to feel OK all at once. Just knowing that life is slowly getting better means that there is light at the end of the tunnel

less often. You could try being active, being with people or doing something you enjoy (even though you might not feel like it).

Talk to someone you trust about your bad thoughts. Saying them out loud for the first time is scary but then starts to make them feel less frightening.

Tell yourself about the good things you've done today instead of the bad things. Some people find that it helps to imagine having a great time with their favourite band or football team or movie star. Or it could be eating your favourite meal or lying on a beach in the sun.

Just thinking about your bad thoughts a bit less often can be a great achievement. It can help you realise that you are starting to win the battle.

If you find it difficult to talk, write it down and send a letter or an e-mail.

Don't be afraid of going to see a specialist like a counsellor or psychiatrist. There are some very good 'talking treatments' which work really well, especially if you go in the early days of feeling unwell. If you are not able to relate to the person you are seeing – ask to see someone else.

Listen to the advice you are being given and act on it.

Try to get help with the problems which may be causing your depression.

If you have been given medication (tablets) to help with your suicidal feelings, make sure you understand how long it takes before they start having an effect. If they don't seem to be working, tell your doctor so that he/she can try something else. Don't stop taking them because you feel better or because you are having side effects. Get advice from your doctor first. You can also talk to your pharmacist about your medication.

Avoid alcohol and drugs. Although at first they give you a lift, they are known to make depressed people feel even worse in the long run. Under their influence you may do things or make decisions you would not normally make. Using alcohol and other drugs can actually make some people suicidal. Even cannabis can have this effect too.

Stop any risk-taking behaviour – where you want the decision as to whether you live or die to be left to chance. Like driving the car in a way that could kill you (or someone else). Don't be pressured into doing risky things by other people.

Be very careful of making an impulsive decision to kill yourself

Don't listen to sad music when you're really down.

Start looking after yourself with regular meals and plenty of exercise. Get out into the daylight and try to stay out of bed until night-time. Find something to do which gives some structure to your day.

Don't expect to feel OK all at once. Just knowing that life is slowly getting better means that there is light at the end of the tunnel.

Make a list, with phone numbers, of people and/or organisations you can turn to for help in a crisis.

■ For more information about PAPYRUS contact us at: Rossendale GH, Union Road, Rawtenstall. BB4 6NE. Phone & Fax 01706 214449 www.papyrus-uk.org e-mail: info@papyrus-uk.org

■ With grateful thanks to the young people of Deeside College, North Wales, the Child and Family Mental Health team at Doncaster Royal Infirmary, and staff at the Royal Liverpool Children's Hospital.

© Papyrus

After suicide

Information from the Compassionate Friends

The death of a child is always devastating, but suicide is a particularly cruel form of death for the surviving family and friends. How can our child have been so full of despair that he or she felt that death was preferable to life? Additionally, the families of children who have completed suicide have to cope with the police, an inquest, and possibly the media, as well as the ever-present and unanswerable question 'Why?'

We hope that by reading about the feelings that others have experienced, and some of the thoughts that have helped them, you will at least feel that you are not alone in your grief. At the end of this article there are details about our support group, Shadow of Suicide (SoS), and other information which may help you to survive.

The early days

Whatever the circumstances surrounding the death, no parent is ever prepared for the suicide of their child. Even for those families who have lived for years with mental illness, repeated attempts at death and their child's lack of belief that the future may be better, the actual death is still a profound shock. For some parents there is no such introduction; the suicide comes out of the blue, the police are at the door telling you something you cannot begin to believe. Some parents may not have seen their child for months or years; for others, their lives were closely entwined and their child lived, and even died, in the family home. Each suicide has its own story which the family must unravel in their own way. The common threads are the feelings: numbness, shock, disbelief, and then the questions. And all this is before the pain of grief and loss truly begins.

The families of children who have completed suicide have to cope with the police, an inquest . . . as well as the ever-present and unanswerable question 'Why?'

Most parents find themselves tormented by unanswered questions and feel a deep need to try to understand why their child killed themselves. For many, there is a huge element of self-blame in these questions: *what did we fail to see? why did he not ask us for help? what support did we not get for her?* Suicide can feel like the ultimate failure of parenting. These feelings can be very painful for close family and friends who can see they are not true or logical, but are nevertheless totally real to the grieving parent. Anger and blame are powerful emotions in these early days. For some people, finding convincing or adequate reasons for the suicide proves elusive, leaving many unanswered questions. While we seek a reason for our child's action (in a broken relationship, inadequate mental health care, bullying, pressure of exams, a lost job, for example) we still ask ourselves, 'how could you do this – to yourself and to us?'

A death by suicide inevitably involves the police, the coroner (procurator fiscal in Scotland) and an inquest, with the possibility of media interest since the coroner's court is open to press and public. The TCF leaflet *On Inquests* (in England and Wales) may be helpful. If there is media interest, it is often a good idea to release a brief statement, together with a photograph of your child, so that accurate information is used. You can then ask them to respect your need for privacy in your

grief. There will be a verdict, which may not agree with the family's understanding of what happened and which may be some months after the event. For a verdict of suicide to be recorded there has to be clear evidence of intent; many suicide deaths, however, are given an open verdict. Some find this helpful, but it can hurt a family wanting honesty, openness and a lack of ambiguity.

The impact on the family

Every death leaves a huge gap; there has been an amputation, someone is missing and can never be replaced. Suicide brings added complications to the bereaved family. Although the days when suicide was regarded as a criminal or sinful act are hopefully in the past, some families do discover how hard it can be to talk openly about suicide, how uncomfortable even close friends can feel about the tragedy, and how this can lead to isolation. There can also be differences, as well as togetherness, even within the immediate family, in the way each person views the past as well as in their interpretation of the death. These different interpretations can be very divisive. Misunderstandings can grow as each parent pursues their own road. Rifts can widen and real estrangement can occur, even between those partners who thought themselves to be close before. Marriages and partnerships do break down in the aftermath of the death of a child, and can be especially vulnerable after a suicide.

It takes great determination and forbearance to hang on during these conflicts, to avoid being destructive, and to respect each other's view of the truth. Those who do manage to survive and stay together sometimes look back at this horrendous period of turbulence and wonder how they came through it together. Support from a close friend, or some professional counselling, may help one or both partners through this time. As well as differing views of past events, there are often major differences in the way we grieve; each partner needs to give the other space, respect and understanding. There may be feelings of anger, blame and guilt as well as grief, and these may create conflict at a time when the

Some families do discover how hard it can be to talk openly about suicide, how uncomfortable even close friends can feel about the tragedy, and how this can lead to isolation

family wants to be able to support one another. Each member of the family will have to make his or her own journey through grief, and eventually come to an understanding of what has happened. Every family is a collection of individuals and many experience the feeling that they are 'together ... but alone'.

It is almost impossible to find a way of explaining suicide to young children, yet it is vital that children do know what is going on, so that they do not feel excluded from the family. While we do not want to burden them with terrible details, it is better that they hear the truth from us rather than in the playground or on television. We do need to find a way of being honest; to avoid saying something they will later discover was a lie or a pretence. We will also want to ensure that others close to the child are giving a similar explanation. Many people feel that the idea of a loved brother or sister deciding to die is not one which a child can or should be expected to understand. Perhaps we should not

try to explain too much; we need to reply honestly to their questions, to hug and to hold, to reassure them that they are loved, that we share their grief. As our children grow older, their understanding of death, and of suicide, will mature and we can talk to them in different language. It is a subject we should not avoid discussing as the years go by and our children approach adulthood.

Older brothers and sisters may find it very hard to share their thoughts and emotions with their parents. They may feel furiously angry at their dead sibling for destroying the family, for leaving them to cope with grief and chaos, or they may blame their parents for not being able to prevent it happening. Yet, though witnessing their parents' grief and not wishing to add to it, they may not feel able to share these thoughts. Great rifts and silences can open up without anyone intending this to happen. Their feeling of isolation can be terrifying. For a few, suicide also brings the dreadful added possibility of following their dead brother or sister, if the pain gets too bad: 'I can always do what they did'. Parents, too, can share this fear and 'watch' their surviving children with anguish, full of foreboding as well as grief, and yet unable to help. It is helpful for the surviving children to have someone they can talk to, and this person will often be outside the immediate family. Parents can make sure that school, the families of close friends, religious and club leaders know what has happened. However painful it is, the family needs to keep sharing and talking, to weep together, and to avoid the trap of suppressing feelings lest they hurt. It will help our children to let them see that we hurt too.

The funeral can be especially demanding when the death has been by suicide. Careful preparation and guidance from sympathetic friends and clergy can help us to focus on our child's life, rather than the manner of his or her death. It can be hard to do this, so near to the actual death, and while our minds are still full of unanswered questions. Each family has to find their own way of creating a funeral that is fitting for their child. (See TCF leaflet *Preparing your child's funeral*).

For a single parent, with or without surviving children, this is a terrible and lonely time. There are special issues, too, for parents whose only child has died and for step-families. You need to let family and friends support you, not turn them away because they cannot understand the true depths of your loss. Help from your child's grieving friends can be a most surprising source of strength, and you may be able to support each other. TCF has leaflets on these special circumstances, and a support network for those who are now childless; details of this group are available from the National Office.

Surviving

As the weeks pass, the inquest takes place, and the family begins to try to pick up the threads of life again. Yet for many the unanswerable questions are still there. There is still a great need to retell our story, to try to piece together the events that led up to the suicide, to talk to those who were involved. Some of us find it a help to write the story of our child's life and death, that doing this brings the multitude of strands into some sort of order and perspective. For those who do not share these needs, this can seem obsessive and unreasonable. Some family members find it easier than others to accept that they can never totally understand another's mind and that we do have to live with partial knowledge. These differences can make grieving together very hard. Friends are often at a loss, not knowing what to say or do, and the bereaved parent will sometimes feel that their friends cannot help because they have not experienced such a disaster in their own lives. Some friends will persist, even when their efforts are rejected, but others may back off, leaving us feeling deserted and betrayed. But we do not have to feel alone.

The lives of parents and families are irreversibly changed by suicide. Some of us have found that counselling can help us through this devastating time

---

The Compassionate Friends (TCF) has a group, Shadow of Suicide, where every family has endured a similarly devastating experience. Sometimes the SoS group is the only lifeline; the bond between a group of parents bereaved by suicide can be very strong. We can share memories of our children, both sad and happy, and can tell our stories as often as we need without fear of rejection or a lack of understanding. Parents meet in various ways: by attending group meetings, by visiting one-to-one, on the telephone, by writing letters, and through TCF's Newsletter. The annual TCF Gathering offers SoS parents a chance to meet others from across the country, perhaps those with whom they have been corresponding, as well as parents bereaved in many other ways.

TCF has a Postal Library with more than 1,000 titles, plus audio and visual tapes. There is a special section on suicide, which many parents find helpful in their quest for understanding. Siblings have their own quarterly newsletter, *SIBBS* (Support In Bereavement for Brothers and Sisters); this often contains letters and articles on suicide and can be an important way for siblings to realise that they, too, are not alone.

The lives of parents and families are irreversibly changed by suicide. Some of us have found that counselling can help us through this devastating time. If you need help choosing a counsellor, ask your doctor, religious leader or local Social Services department for advice.

At first, and often for some time, it seems impossible even to imagine finding peace of mind and heart. However, almost imperceptibly over the months and years, adjustment does come and it is possible to rebuild our lives and to move forward, carrying with us our love for our child. We must give ourselves time to heal the deep wound and to learn to survive.

■ The above information is from the Compassionate Friends' web site which can be found at www.tcf.org.uk

© *The Compassionate Friends*

Survivors of bereavement by suicide

The survivor of a suicide bereavement faces a stark choice . . . 'It is up to you . . . to decide whether to be permanently hurt by the last act of a free individual or not . . . this option is YOURS' (Lake 1984).

- Know you can survive. You may not think so but you can.
- Struggle with 'why' it happened until you no longer need to know 'why' or until you are satisfied with partial answers.
- Know you may feel overwhelmed by the intensity of your feelings, but all these feelings are normal.
- You may feel rejected, abandoned, share these feelings.
- Anger, guilt, confusion, denial, forgetfulness are common responses. You are not going crazy; you are in mourning. Be aware you may feel anger, appropriate anger, at the person, at the world, at friends, at God, at yourself; it is all right to express it.
- You may feel guilty for what you think you did or did not do. Remember the choice was not yours – one cannot be responsible for another's actions.
- Find a good listener; be open and honest about your feelings.
- Do not remain silent – about what has happened or about how you feel.
- You may feel suicidal, this is normal, it does not mean you will act on those thoughts.
- Do not be afraid to cry, tears are healing.
- Keeping an emotional diary is useful as well as healing. Record your thoughts, feelings and behaviour. Writing a letter to the deceased expressing your thoughts and feelings can also be part of the healing process.
- Give yourself time to heal.
- Expect setbacks. If emotions return like a tidal wave, you may be experiencing 'unfinished business'.
- Try to put off making any major decisions.
- Seek professional advice. Be aware of the pain of your family and friends.
- Be patient with yourself and with others who may not understand.
- Set your own limits and learn to say no.
- Ask questions, work through the guilt, anger, bitterness and other feelings until you can let them go. Letting go does not mean forgetting.
- It is common to experience physical symptoms in your grief, headaches, sleeplessness, loss of appetite etc.
- Know that you will never be the same again, but you can survive and even go beyond just surviving.

SOBS (Survivors Of Bereavement by Suicide) is a self-help, voluntary organisation. Many of those helping have, themselves, been bereaved by suicide.

We exist to meet the needs and break the isolation of those bereaved by the suicide of a close relative or friend.

We offer emotional and practical support in a number of ways:

- Telephone contacts
- Bereavement packs
- Group meetings (in a number of locations)
- One-day conferences
- Residential events
- Information relating to practical issues and problems

Our aim is to provide a safe, confidential environment in which bereaved people can share their experiences and feelings, so giving and gaining support from each other.

We also strive to improve public awareness and maintain contacts with many other statutory and voluntary organisations.

Suicide recognises no age, social, ethnic or cultural boundaries – neither do we. Our groups are open to any individual or family.

We are a self-help organisation and are always looking for people to help with our groups and Helpline – contact us if you feel you have the time and inclination to assist.

Bereaved by suicide. You don't have to face it alone. National Helpline 0870 241 3337. Available 9am – 9pm every day

KEY FACTS

■ Suicide and attempted suicide are often linked to a build-up, or combination of difficult events. There might also be a 'last straw' event that encourages someone to attempt suicide. (p. 01)

■ Suicide is three times as common in men than women and the number of suicides among young men has increased dramatically over the last 10 years. (p. 01)

■ An estimated 815,000 people killed themselves in 2000 – a rate of 14.5 per 100,000 or roughly one death every 40 seconds. (p. 02)

■ Groups particularly at risk of suicide include unemployed or homeless young people, young gay men and women, and young people who have problems with drugs. (p. 05)

■ Anyone who talks about killing himself or herself, or tries to do it, is deeply unhappy, and needs help. (p. 05)

■ People self-harm because they are in pain and trying to cope. They could also be trying to show that something is wrong. They need to be taken seriously. (p. 08)

■ Self-harm can be very frightening and difficult to deal with, so people who work with children need training and support to help them respond sensitively and well. (p. 09)

■ Like anorexia it has a higher prevalence in teenagers and young people. Also like anorexia it is more commonly experienced by women than by men. The best estimate is 1 in 130 people – 446,000 or nearly half a million across the UK. (p. 10)

■ The most common form of self-injury is probably cutting, usually superficially, but sometimes deeply. Women may also burn themselves, punch themselves or hit their bodies against something. Some people pick their skin or pull out hair. (p. 12)

■ About 1.5 million people in the UK deliberately inflict some form of injury on themselves every year – with 10,000 needing hospital treatment – and increasing numbers are mutilating their own bodies as a way of releasing emotional pain. Disturbingly, the majority are women. (p. 12)

■ In 1997 to 1998, the last year for which there is available data, there were 178 suicides or undetermined deaths among students. (p. 15)

■ About 5,000 people commit suicide in England each year. It is the commonest cause of death in men under 35 and the main cause of premature death among people with mental illness. (p. 16)

■ The government's current target is a 20% reduction in the number of suicides by 2010. (p. 18)

■ In Scotland there were 887 suicides in 2001 – a 22 per cent increase over the last 20 years. The rate of increase is one of the highest in Europe. The rate for males is almost three times that for females. For young females, the number of those in their early teens being treated for self-harm is also a cause for concern. (p. 20)

■ If someone cuts themselves, they might not be suicidal. Many young people use this behaviour as a way of feeling in control. They are still in need of good friends and might want someone to talk to, someone who isn't going to say they're going mad. (p. 21)

■ 'Although suicides at certain institutions have always interested the media, rates of suicide among students are no higher than among the general population. In fact, evidence suggests the suicide rate in students is lower than that in the age-matched population, but this does not mean we can afford to be complacent.' (p. 22)

■ Most suicidal people don't actually want to die, but are looking for an answer to their problems, an end to their pain and despair. Suicide can seem the only way out. It is a decision made when other decisions seem impossible. (p. 23)

■ It's important to make sure that the young person feels that they have someone they can talk to and get support from when they need it. (p. 25)

■ When self-injury becomes a way of coping with stress it is a sign that there are problems that need sorting out. Help or support may be needed from family, friends, or others. (p. 27)

■ More than 24,000 teenagers are taken to hospital in Britain each year after deliberately harming themselves, mostly through drug overdoses or cutting themselves. (p. 29)

■ Suicide among young people is a phenomenon both puzzling and worrying. The rates of male suicide in all age groups and in most countries have shown a striking increase since the 1970s but this is most marked in the 15 to 24 year age group. (p. 32)

■ Sometimes the person who attempts suicide does not die but damages their body so badly that full recovery is impossible. (p. 34)

■ Don't expect to feel OK all at once. Just knowing that life is slowly getting better means that there is light at the end of the tunnel. (p. 35)

■ The families of children who have completed suicide have to cope with the police, an inquest . . . as well as the ever-present and unanswerable question 'Why?' (p. 36)

ADDITIONAL RESOURCES

You might like to contact the following organisations for further information. Due to the increasing cost of postage, many organisations cannot respond to enquiries unless they receive a stamped, addressed envelope.

Befrienders International
c/o Samaritans
Upper Mill, Kingston Road
Ewell, Surrey
Tel: 020 8541 4949
Fax: 020 54915448
E-mail: admin@befrienders.org
Web site: www.befrienders.org

Bristol Crisis Service for Women
PO Box 654
Bristol, BS99 1XH
Tel; 0117 927 9600
Fax: 0117 925 1119
E-mail: bcsw@womens-crisis-
service.freeserve.co.uk
Web site: www.users.zetnet.co.uk/
bcsw/

CALM (Campaign Against Living Miserably)
Skipton House
London, SE1 6LH
Tel: 020 7972 5275
Web site: www.thecalmzone.net/

ChildLine
45 Folgate Street
London, E1 6GL
Tel: 020 7650 3200
Fax: 020 7650 3201
reception@childline.org.uk
Web site: www.childline.org.uk

Compassionate Friends
53 North Street
Bristol, BS3 1EN
Tel: 0117 966 5202
Fax: 0117 914 4368
E-mail: info@tcf.org.uk
Web site: www.tcf.org.uk

Mental Health Foundation
7th Floor
83 Victoria Street
London, SW1H 0HW
Tel: 020 7802 0300
Fax: 020 7802 0301
E-mail: mhf@mhf.org.uk
Web site:
www.mentalhealth.org.uk

National Youth Agency (NYA)
17-23 Albion Street
Leicester, LE1 6GD
Tel: 0116 285 3700
Fax: 0116 285 3777
E-mail: nya@nya.org.uk
Web site: www.nya.org.uk

NCH
85 Highbury Park
London, N5 1UD
Tel: 020 7704 7000
Fax: 020 7226 2537
Web site: www.nch.org.uk

Papyrus-Prevention of Suicides
Rossendale G H
Union Road
Rawtenstall, BB4 6NE
Tel: 01706 214449
Fax: 01706 214449
E-mail: infoweb2@papyrus-uk.org
Web site: www.papyrus-uk.org

Royal College of Psychiatrists
17 Belgrave Square
London, SW1X 8PG
Tel: 020 7235 2351
Fax: 020 7235 1935
E-mail: rcpsych@rcpsych.ac.uk
Web site: www.rcpsych.ac.uk

Self-Harm Alliance
PO Box 61
Cheltenham, GL51 8YB
Tel: 01242 578820
E-mail: selfharmalliance@aol.com
Web site:
www.selfharmalliance.org

Survivors of Bereavement by Suicide (SOBS)
Centre 88
Saner Street
Hull, HU3 2TR
Tel: 01482 610728
Fax: 01482 210287
Web site: www.uk-sobs.org.uk

The Basement Project
The Self-Injury Forum
PO Box 5
Abergavenny
NP7 5XW
Tel: 01873 856524
E-mail:
basement.project@virgin.net
freespace.virgin.net/
basement.project/default.htm

The Samaritans
The Upper Mill
Kingston Road
Ewell, Surrey, KT17 2AF
Tel: 020 8394 8300
Fax: 020 8394 8301
E-mail: admin@samaritans.org.uk
Web site: www.samaritans.org.uk

World Health Organization (WHO)
20 Avenue Appia
1211-Geneva 27
SWITZERLAND
Tel: + 41 22 791 2111
Fax: + 41 22 791 3111
E-mail: info@who.ch
Web site: www.who.int

YoungMinds
102-108 Clerkenwell Road
London, EC1M 5SA
Tel: 020 7336 8445
Fax: 020 7336 8446
E-mail:
enquiries@youngminds.org.uk
Web site: www.youngminds.org.uk

INDEX

ACKNOWLEDGEMENTS

The publisher is grateful for permission to reproduce the following material.

While every care has been taken to trace and acknowledge copyright, the publisher tenders its apology for any accidental infringement or where copyright has proved untraceable. The publisher would be pleased to come to a suitable arrangement in any such case with the rightful owner.

Chapter One: Self-harm and Suicide

Suicide, © 2003 National Youth Agency, *Self-directed violence*, © World Health Organization (WHO), *Worldwide suicide rates*, © World Health Organization (WHO), *The warning signs of suicide*, © Befrienders International, *Suicide*, © ChildLine, *Girls who cut*, © Hilary Freeman, *Self-harm: the facts*, © The Basement Project, *Injuries*, © NCH, *Shock figures*, © NCH, *Self-harm*, © Mental Health Foundation, *Myth breaking*, © Self Harm Alliance, *Women and self-injury*, © Bristol Crisis Service for Women, *Self-harm*, © National Magazine Company Limited.

Chapter Two: Seeking Help

Guiding light, © Guardian Newspapers Limited 2003, *Sources of help following suicide attempts*, © Crown copyright is reproduced with the permission of Her Majesty's Stationery Office, *Suicide prevention strategy*, © Guardian Newspapers Limited 2003, *Stigma ties*, © Angela Lambert, *Lifetime suicide attempts*, © Crown copyright is reproduced with the permission of Her Majesty's Stationery Office, *Living on the edge*, © Crown copyright is reproduced with the permission of Her Majesty's Stationery Office, *Death rates from suicide by gender and age*, © Crown copyright is reproduced with the permission of Her Majesty's Stationery Office, *First suicide prevention strategy launched*, © Crown copyright is reproduced with the permission of Her Majesty's Stationery Office, *If a friend is suicidal*, © Papyrus, *Fight for survival*, © Kate Coxon, *Suicide*, © CALM, *Deliberate self-harm in young people*, © Royal College of Psychiatrists, *Type and reasons for deliberate self-harm*, © Crown copyright is reproduced with the permission of Her Majesty's Stationery Office, *Treating the stigma*, © Guardian Newspapers Limited 2003, *Worried about self-injury?*, © YoungMinds, *One in ten teenagers self-harm*, © Guardian Newspapers Limited 2003, *Self-harm in schools*, © Basement Project, *Young men speak*, © Samaritans, *Family conflict*, © Samaritans, *Thinking of ending it all?*, © Papyrus, Social functioning characteristics, © Crown copyright is reproduced with the permission of Her Majesty's Stationery Office, *After suicide*, © Compassionate Friends, *Survivors of bereavement by suicide*, © Survivors of bereavement by suicide (SOBS).

Photographs and illustrations:

Pages 1, 11, 20, 27, 30, 38: Simon Kneebone; pages 5, 18, 24, 36: Pumpkin House; pages 6, 12, 22, 31, 39: Bev Aisbett.

Craig Donnellan
Cambridge
January, 2004